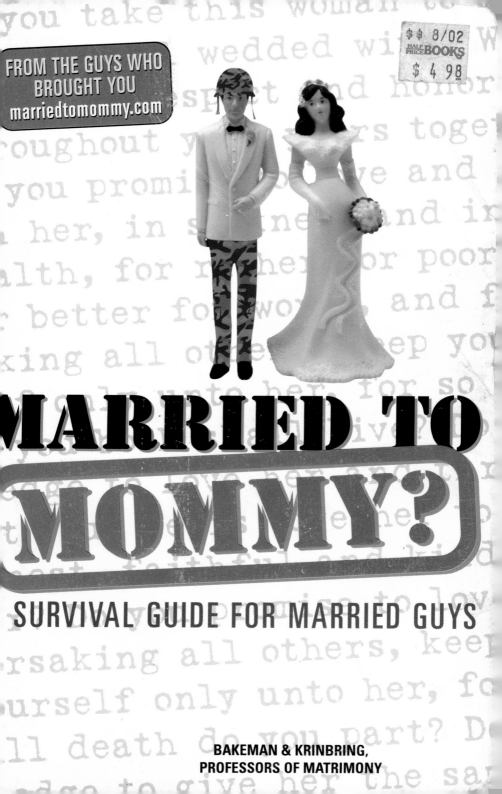

FROM THE GUYS WHO
BROUGHT YOU
marriedtomommy.com

MARRIED TO
MOMMY?

SURVIVAL GUIDE FOR MARRIED GUYS

BAKEMAN & KRINBRING,
PROFESSORS OF MATRIMONY

MARRIED TO

MOMMY?

A SURVIVAL GUIDE FOR MARRIED GUYS

**BAKEMAN & KRINBRING,
PROFESSORS OF MATRIMONY**

PULP!

P.O. Box 70584
Seattle WA 98107
1-877-723-7857

Design by Lab51

Printed in the United States of America

ABOUT THE AUTHORS

With over 53 years of marital experience between them, the authors of this book truly are "Professors Of Matrimony."

Brian Krinbring lives with his family in Seattle, Washington, and carries on his studies of matrimony from the husband and father level. It is at this level that he's developed such a keen understanding of what marriage is all about. It is interesting to note, however, that his wife Sue is not a Mommy. Professor Krinbring has learned about Mommies from friends and neighbors.

Jeff Bakeman lives with his family on Whidbey Island, just north of Seattle. His first-hand knowledge of marriage comes from his experience at "hand-to-hand marriage." A veteran of 21 years of wedded bliss, Professor Bakeman, strangely, is also not married to a Mommy. He does, however, know some guys who are, and it is from these contacts that he's developed his insightful viewpoints, experiments and tutorials.

The Professors work as a team, counseling married guys via phone, email, or even fax. Personal counsel can be obtained every Friday night from 5 P.M. to 7 P.M. at various bars in and around Seattle. These sessions are commonly referred to as "Beer Fridays," where guys are welcome, but Mommies are not allowed.

You can contact the Professors directly at www.marriedtomommy.com.

ACKNOWLEDGEMENTS

The Professors would like to thank Rew and Amy from PULP! and Stephen Michaud for their support and invaluable assistance. In addition, they would like to give special thanks to the multitude of Mommies out there, without whom this book would never have been written.

CONTENTS

Introduction   v

Chapter 1   The Best of Times   1

Chapter 2   A Fighting Chance   7

Chapter 3   The Mommy Trap: A Test   15

Chapter 4   Avoiding Conflict   23

Chapter 5   Learning to Listen   31

Chapter 6   You Have a Friend in Vagueness   35

Chapter 7   AAQWAQ   41

Chapter 8   On Being Late   45

Chapter 9   Work: Making It Work for You   55

Chapter 10   Home-o'-phobia   67

Chapter 11   The "Honey-Do" List   75

Chapter 12   Sports   83

Chapter 13   Cooking for Mommy   91

Chapter 14   Pouching Your Dollars   99

Chapter 15   Imaginary Friends   105

Chapter 16   Her Four Special Days   109

Chapter 17   Fire and Sex   127

Chapter 18   The Eleven Types of Married Sex   131

             Afterword: A Brighter Future   141

INTRODUCTION

She was different. He'd never met a woman like her before.

They ate late night dinners at trendy restaurants and took spontaneous weekend trips. They jogged together and played golf together. One night she knocked on his apartment door with strawberries, whipped cream, and champagne wearing nothing but a trench coat. About once a week she'd invite him to her office for lunch—and lock the door. On a warm summer evening they took a private hot air balloon ride and she made him a member of the mile high club before they were five hundred feet off the ground!

In a quasi-delusional trance, he mumbled… "I do."

That was two years ago. He has since spent his entire savings on expensive fertility drugs and procedures, and she's become a proud mother. She quit her high-paying job and they moved from Seattle to his new job, where he now works six days a week. His golf clubs are rusting in the basement, champagne has become too expensive, strawberries are out of season and the trench coat doesn't quite fit. To top it off, there are no balloon rides in Cleveland. She was different alright.

True story. All of it. In many ways it's every married guy's story.

What Happened?

As Professors of Matrimony, we have shined our flashlights of inquiry into the darkest corners of the post nuptial netherworld to expose what happens to a man, and especially a woman, once the knot is tied.

The reality is: Men don't change. Not much anyway. Women, on the other hand, experience a sort of marital metamorphosis. Nearly all of them turn into what we call "Mommies"—a state of being really; an attitude with a capital A; a point of view. In many ways it's as if the butterfly bride crawled back into her cocoon and re-emerged as a caterpillar!

This book will provide insight to better understand this weird yet predictable transformation and give the tools to deal with it. Applied properly, these tools will make marriage better for both of you, even fun! Then you too can become a Licensed Practicing Husband like us—happily *Married to Mommy*.

CHAPTER 1
The Best of Times

*"She had a face that would let her get away,
He saw that face and he lost all control..."*

—BOB SEGER

*"Tiger will definitely not get married before
he's 30; a woman can do a lot of damage to a
man's golf game."*

—EARL WOODS

We've all been there. Remember those first dates? When you "got some" on her front porch until one of her parents turned on the lights to shoo you away? Everything about her seemed magical. Those are fond memories. They are also something to learn from. That was the first time a harmless-sounding thing known as "feminine wiles" got the better of you. That was when the evolutionary power of women began to blind you. Many of us haven't seen the light of day since.

You see, during those innocent teenage years, after the heavy breathing was over for the night, she went upstairs, and made an entry in her diary:

Could he be the one? He's so sweet in a clumsy sort of way. How can I get him to ask me to the prom?

Then, the dewy object of your aching desire would start combining your name with hers:

Julie Moss-Flaventrap

Mrs. John Flaventrap

Julie, John Jr, and April Flaventrap

The Flaventraps

She was upstairs at her house planning **your** future!

You, on the other hand, were home in the shower with your reliable bar of Irish Spring, visions of lust running through your head.

And you haven't changed much since. Puberty pretty well establishes the limits of the male personality. But many women—and it is impossible to predict which ones—seem to metamorphose over time from sexy, long-haired girlfriends, to earnest wives, and inexorably into... **Mommies!**

Does this occur by chance? Emphatically, no.

The transformation is programmed, and pre-meditated. In fact, it really isn't a transformation at all. When young women reach the predator stage of their development they suppress their real selves, and certainly their agendas. Wolves do not talk to pigs of pork chops and ham.

This charade is nowhere better presented than in the best-selling book, *The Rules*. Authors Ellen Fein and Sherrie Schneider are full of hints how to play out the feminine masquerade to *capture* a man. Hints like: "Be easy to live with," "Don't tell him what to do," "Be feminine, grow your hair long," and "Wear black panty hose and hike up your skirt to entice." In one particularly telling passage, they advise women to become "a creature unlike any other." Once married, women become creatures all right—a creature known as Mommy!

We use the term "Mommy" because it perfectly defines the persona that far too many women take on after just a few short years of marriage. Generally uptight, perpetually practical, and constantly striving to be in control of everything—all the time—the dreadnought Mommy is truly a marital force to be reckoned with.

Remember how dating was all about fun? It didn't matter if you stayed out late, or how many beers you had, or if she rode on the back of your motorcycle without a helmet. She did *everything* you wanted to do. Ever so slowly, the Mommy inside began to emerge as you were blindly marched through the cattle chute of engagement to the sausage grinder of marriage.

The Mommy transformation is usually complete within a few years, and almost always by the time the children arrive. For example, if a newlywed tracks dirt on the carpet, he is lovingly forgiven as if he's made cute little puppy-dog-footprints. Within a few short years those same footprints become an *irresponsible act of transgression.* The honeymooner starts out like a frisky little puppy looking for affection with his slobbery puppy breath "kisses." All too soon, however, he becomes a BAD DOG, who is told "you smell like a brewery and just might as well forget about it."

What a woeful devolution it is. When you were younger you took the short-term, tactical view and focused on two central questions: **How can I get laid? And, how can I get laid—NOW?** Your Mommy-in-the-making may have obliged you, even encouraged you, but that was because her long-range radar was tracking USS Marriage. Seemingly spontaneous sex was her way of neutralizing the target vessel—you.

Once married, however, a true Mommy's long-range radar shuts down—the target has been secured—and her local scanner kicks in. To her, the important questions now become: "Is Charmin really better than the economy one-ply?" and, "Are we ready to make the move from one percent to skim?"

A sort of role reversal occurs. You are forced to set aside your recurring dilemma—"How can I get laid, now?" Instead you must glumly refocus on distant targets, cosmic issues such as 30-year mortgage rates, the looming cost of college in the 21st Century, and finding an answer to a new recurring question: **What happened?**

Guys don't mind if Mommy doesn't share the tedium of their long-term strategic thinking. But woe be the husband who does not at least feign interest in the day-to-day details of homelife. Bring home the wrong brand of diapers, or mistakenly purchase crunchy instead of creamy peanut butter, and the Supreme Court, constantly in session in Mommy's mind, will condemn you of not caring about her, the kids, or the marriage. No amount of explanation will post your bail.

Not all women are 100% Mommies. But there's a little Mommy lurking inside every wife. It may be genetic. It may be the water. No matter it's cause, the important thing for you to realize is that you'll probably be married most of your adult life, possibly until it kills you.

The gravity of the situation is shown by the graph below:

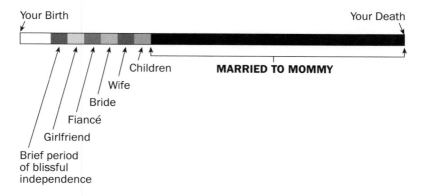

Your Birth

Your Death

Children

MARRIED TO MOMMY

Wife

Bride

Fiancé

Girlfriend

Brief period
of blissful
independence

CHAPTER 2

A Fighting Chance

"This is my thumbnail sketch of marriage:
A woman sees a man; she likes him. Now, she
jumps on this thing and rides it to some kind of a
standstill. Then she changes it and trains it, and to
the exact degree that she's able to do this, she
disrespects him."

—JACK NICHOLSON

When a guy gets married, he conceives of the union with simple logic:

A. She's kinda fun.

B. I like sex with her. If I get married I'll get more.

C. All my friends are getting married.

D. If I don't get married now, I could end up wasting my life in front of the tube, scratching my balls and eating fried pork rinds.

An aspiring Mommy, by contrast, approaches marriage in far more encompassing terms. She wants more. She wants *all* of you. If you're not careful she will take:

Your time

Your money

Your power

Your self-respect

Your man-seed

And ultimately... your fun

That's why this book is about nothing less than SELF PRESERVATION.

Don't presume guys can win. We can't. It's best to simply try to improve the odds to the point where there's at least a fighting chance of survival. Yes, we're talking survival here, because it has always been, and always will be, a battle to the death. A battle the male of the species usually loses. Check out the actuarial tables. The average woman outlives the average man by seven years!

Know also that we've never had the upper hand. Some guys may believe they were actually in charge when *they*, not she, called to make that infamous first date. Not a chance! To believe you have ever exercised any meaningful control in your relationship is to miss two important points—one obvious, one more subtle:

1. **From the beginning, she had the power because she could say "yes" or "no" to going out with you.**
   But you say… "I'm still the one in charge because I showed the initiative and called her."

That brings us to Point Two, the subtle one:

2. **The reason you called her in the first place is because *she wanted you to call her.***
   It's true! She culled you from your herd of beer-drinking swine like a hungry lioness does with a weak, confused wildebeest.

This occurs because of the Overriding Fact of Life:

MEN LOVE WOMEN MORE THAN WOMEN LOVE MEN!

Our studies have found four major reasons for this:

1. **Men are more physically attracted to women than women are to men.**
   Men see women as fragile creatures of beauty with soft, rounded curves, smooth hairless skin and delicate features—something that innately looks like it should be handled with care.

   Men, on the other hand, are generally hairy, have big noses, and fart a lot. Because of this, it is easier for a woman to ream a man. Why not? He's just an ugly brute, he can take it—in fact, he's so ugly, he deserves it!

2. **Men love their wives more than their children, but women love their children more than their husbands.**
Most guys have a vague notion of this upon entering marriage, but the concept of children is so foreign that we suppress our fears and soldier onward. At least we can take solace in the fact that we don't end up like our less-fortunate insect brethren, Mr. Praying Mantis and Mr. Black Widow.

3. **Men love women as they are, women love men as "fixer-uppers."**
A man meets a woman and within a few short moments he knows if he likes her… just the way she is. A woman, on the other hand, pre-qualifies her prospect. Before a pre-Mommy decides to fall in love, she will need to know about his family, his social status, his religion, his friends, his job, his "potential." Once he's all checked out, it's head-over-heels time! After the head goes over the heels, Mommy begins her unending crusade to ensure her newly-acquired husband reaches the potential she just *knows* is locked up inside.

4. **Men need women for sexual fulfillment more than women need men.**
The clean fresh scent of Irish Spring just doesn't stand up well over time.

In fact, any woman can get a man, anytime she likes. One has to look no further than Wallis Simpson, Evita Perón, or Monica Lewinski to understand this point. Contrary to what the feminists may say, it's women—not men—who have all the power. If you don't believe us, answer this question: Can you get a woman anytime you like?

The scariest thing is they can turn it on and off at will! In an article written by John Tiernay for *New York Times Magazine,* he quotes anthropologist Margaret Mead's observation that women can "temper their sexual impulses with a thousand other considerations, such as winning and keeping a lover or husband, or balancing the mood of the moment against the mood of tomorrow."

Tiernay cites a reinforcing statement from Rutgers anthropologist Helen Tisher: "The human female is the very pinnacle of hormonal self-control."

We don't have a snowball's chance; and according to Tierney, we never have. He believes there's an evolutionary logic behind a woman's ability to subordinate her sex drive:

> "The most successful mothers, the ones whose genetic traits survive today, would be women with good providers faithfully at their side. According to this theory, being discreet about when she was fertile would help a woman keep her partner from straying."

"By hiding any overt signals of her fertility, a female kept the male guessing," agrees William F. Allman, author of *The Stone Age Present.* "The male had to stick around all the time to court her and ward off advances from other men. The longer he stuck around, the more help the woman obtained for herself and her child."

Women have been playing us for suckers for millions of years. And they still are today, right here in America. Look at the facts: Women have 50% of the wealth, represent 52% of the population, and control 100% of the pussy. Yet they have managed to get themselves classified as a minority! Again we're left to ask...*What happened?*

Do you still doubt the power of women? Even Monica was hotter than she thought:

Monica gave President Bill a blowjob,

which

resulted in Big Al not using the President in his campaign,

which

caused Mr. Gore to lose a number of states that he easily could have won,

which

gave Dubya the Presidency,

which

allowed Dubya to nominate environmental-rapist Mommy Gale Norton as Secretary of the Interior,

which

will give her the power to open up millions of acres of heretofore pristine wilderness to oil drilling, which

means cheaper fuel,

which

will allow all the gas-guzzling, air-polluting, supersized-SUV-driving Mommies to keep those road hogs longer and drive them further,

which

combined with the extra pollution caused by all the new oil rigs burning off their excess gas with mile-high flames straight into the wild blue yonder, will burn an even bigger hole in the ozone,

which

will create more global warming,

which

will raise the temperature of the entire planet by 6.9 degrees!

If you still believe men are more powerful than women, answer this question: With a single physical act lasting no more than five minutes, could you raise the temperature of the entire planet?

CHAPTER 3

The Mommy Trap: A Test

*"A man in love is incomplete until he has married.
Then he is finished."*

—ZSA ZSA GABOR

*"The deck is stacked against you and your wife is
holding all the cards."*

—DEAR ABBY

President Reagan often called
his wife, Nancy, "Mommy." Your dad probably called your
mom "Mother" at times. Many men after a few years of
marriage begin to openly refer to their wives as "Mother"
or "Mom."

What the Hell Is Going On Here?

It's a natural inclination for women to be Mommy-like. After
all, it's what they do. Millions of years of evolution have
prepared them for the job. The problem comes when Daddy
allows, and sometimes unwittingly encourages, this smothering
behavior to anesthetize and ultimately destroy him. Like the

frog immersed in the pot of water slowly warming to a boil, guys are often cooked before they know it.

We call this the "Mommy Trap." The reason it's referred to as a "trap" is because it feels pretty good at the start and ends up being a living hell!

It's easy for guys to let their wives do more and more Mommy-like things, but this is a very slippery slope which leads inexorably to total abdication of both power and persona. Oh, the slide down feels good but there's a trap at the bottom that will ensnare you, and emasculate you just like it did your father and his father before him.

As he slides into The Trap, the naïve newlywed will think he's died and gone to heaven. Not only does he have his sexy girlfriend all wrapped up, she now seems to be catering to his every whim! Playing to the fundamentally indolent instincts of men, a Mommy's behavior is like a warm, familiar fog. With time however, the dew point drops, the fog grows thick and cold, and becomes a damp, cloistering blanket of overattention.

Why would Mommy cater to your every whim? Because she loves you? Maybe. But, it's also just another way that a Mommy can exert her power to control "everything, all the time" in her attempt to domesticate you into an herbivore.

You see, guys are an evolved mix of two distinctly different types of creatures: dependent, cud-chewing herbivores and independent, self-reliant carnivores. In most men there is a natural balance of both.

Pre-Mommies go husband hunting with the knowledge that a man with a strong carnivorous side will most likely be a good provider. Once he's caged, Mommies are compelled to tame and domesticate the dangerous beast into herbivorosity.

A clever Mommy will not obliterate the beast. Instead, she simply redirects his carnivorous side toward the business world, unleashing his energy to most benefit her and the brood. Then she "house breaks" the herbivore within him to make sure he brings home the bacon that's been won in the business jungle.

Many a good man has unwittingly slid down the slope into the Mommy Trap of herbivorosity. Next time you get together at a party, look around at the timid, vacant eyes and see how many of your buddies are terminally tangled in The Trap.

"How about another beer?" you'll ask one of them.

"Sounds Great!," he'll reply, looking sheepishly at his Mommy for approval.

Then she'll give him *the look* and he'll say, "On second thought, it's getting late, we gotta go."

Since he's been a good boy, he'll think sex is on the agenda when he gets home—only to find out from Mommy when they do arrive home that it's... "too late."

A Test

Because there's a little Mommy in *all* wives, we've provided this handy test. It will help you determine the magnitude of Mommy you married and the level at which you are a co-conspirator in your own domestication. Keep track of how many warning signs make you grimace and consult our advice at the end.

Warning Sign #1:

Past   Did your mom cook meals for you when you were a kid?

Present   Does your wife cook most of the time now?

Warning Sign #2:

Past   Did your mom do the laundry and iron for you when you were a kid?

Present   Who does the laundry now?

Warning Sign #3:

Past   Did she wear sexy panties before you were married?

Present   What does she wear now?
see essay on no-nonsense pantyhose

Warning Sign #4:

Past   Did your mom buy clothes for you when you were a kid?

Present   Who buys most of your clothes now?

Warning Sign #5:

Past	Did your mom tell you what time you were expected home when you went out for the evening with your high school buddies?
Present	Are you still working with a "curfew?"

Warning Sign#6:

Past	Did your mom have short hair?
Present	Has your wife cut her hair yet? *see essay on short-haired Mommies*

Warning Sign#7:

Past	Was your mom's tone of voice more important than the content of her message?
Present	Do you get that "tone" now?

Warning Sign #8:

Past	Did your mom get after you for "dilly-dallying?"
Present	Does your wife use terms like "lollygagging" or "dawdling" when describing your behavior?

Warning Sign #9:

Present	Do you have children?

SCORING: *How many warning signs apply to you?*

1= Lucky man! You have a "Minor Mommy." Read this book to help you maintain this low score and enjoy a happy, healthy married life.

2–5= Too bad. You are dealing with a "Major Mommy." You will derive great benefits from reading this book and adhering to its teachings.

6+= Holy Kokomo! You are being swamped by a Tsunami Mommy! Head for high ground!

The Short-Haired Mommy

Why do so many women cut their hair after having kids? Not only do many of them fail to return to their pre-pregnancy shape, they compound the problem by cutting their hair!

Here's the standard progression of steps.

1. She takes a pee in the early morning hours and the pregnancy test litmus paper turns blue! You act surprised, excited, and supportive, all the while wondering your recurring question...*What happened?*

2. After all the morning sickness and "showers," the baby arrives.

3. For the first couple of months all is well. Your wife is totally distracted by the baby and you have some time to yourself.

4. Without warning, a sudden cataclysmic change occurs. She's cut off her HAIR! It's so different and, well, so short!

5. You ask, "Why?" She says something like, "With the baby *and all*, it's just easier."

Easier? What does that mean? When you were dating, her hair was a joy to her. It was fun and sexy for her to get her hair ready. Ready for you! It was almost foreplay! Now the hair is gone because it's "easier" and you are relegated to the nowhereland of *"and all."* Once you were her dashing groom, then a responsible, loving husband. Now you're merely a conjunctive phrase.

The slide accelerates and the ties continue to bind...

*No Nonsense?

Speaking of *binding*, did you know that the most successful brand of pantyhose in the world is called "NO NONSENSE?" Think about that name for a moment: No Nonsense! They could have named them anything. How about Party Time Pantyhose? Good Time Pantyhose? Sexybitch Pantyhose? Easy-On, Easy-Off Pantyhose? No. Out of all the zillions of great possibilities they chose "No Nonsense." Why did they do that? In a word—Mommies.

It is a chilling testimony to the all-pervasive power of Mommydom that this has occurred and gone both unnoticed and undealt with by men. When you and your Mommy-in-waiting were dating, it was ALL nonsense. Back then, her underwear of choice ranged from nothing at all to, at most, bikini-cut panties. Now the closest thing to her pleasure patch has a big sign hanging on it: "NO NONSENSE!"

Guys should have been up in arms years ago. Hell, we threw a trade embargo on Iraq for less than that. Instead, we are left sitting on the sexual sidelines, pondering the perennial question: What happened?

As bad as this is, it gets worse. It's usually just a few short years before she starts jamming herself into something called "No Nonsense Control Top–Queen Size." At that point, it's usually so bad that most guys actually look back on the early years of the No Nonsense era with a certain wistful yearning.

CHAPTER 4
Avoiding Conflict

*"The way to fight a woman is with your hat—
grab it and run."*

—JOHN BARRYMORE

*"My wife and I tried breakfast together, but we had
to stop or our marriage would have been ruined."*

—WINSTON CHURCHILL

Smart guys avoid conflict in their marriages like Dracula avoids the rising sun.

This is ironic because men are supposed to be the aggressors. Little boys play more aggressively than do little girls. That's why, the child psychologists tell us, boys are more likely to fight. Even the nursery-school rhymes reinforce this. Boys are "snakes and snails and puppy dog tails," and girls are "sugar and spice and everything nice." Yet when married to Mommy, grown men often become Conflict Avoiders. What happened?

What has escaped the notice of the psycho-scientific community until now is the transformation which takes place in men when they utter those five fateful little words, " 'Til death do us part."

At this point, the noble and valiant carnivore spirit inside a man starts to flag, and he begins his inevitable adaptation into a Conflict Avoider.

Why does this happen? In a word: Mommy.

How are Mommies able to do this? Three reasons:

1. Mommies are more determined and can endure more, therefore they win most of the time.

2. Men fear the long jail sentence that results from taking the " 'Til death do us part" clause too literally.

3. And, **most importantly, MOMMIES KEEP SCORE FOREVER!**

We're not talking game-by-game scores, or even season-by-season, we're talking *lifetime* batting average! And the game is played from the utterance of "I do", 24–7, three hundred sixty friggin' five, until she probates your will and gives away your golf clubs.

Think of those sports trivia junkies who know how many triples Lou Gehrig hit, lifetime, or the date of Warren Spahn's first major league balk. They memorize really obscure stuff, and then enjoy arguing with other stat nuts over whose recollection is correct.

Mommies are just like that, only the statistics they keep are on *you*! Not your wins, mind you, or your home runs or brilliant defensive plays. No sir. Mommies keep particularly accurate stats on your errors, losses, and your embarrassing screw ups. For example, Ty Cobb's lifetime batting average was .367, the highest ever. To his score-keeping Mommy, however, his average was a **minus** .633. Mommies remember everything you have ever done wrong, and they remember it *forever.*

You can't fight that. The prudent male avoids any circumstance in which Mommy can access her internal 100 gigabyte hard drive crammed full of his screw-ups to further leverage her arguments. If he doesn't, she'll resurrect his past failures and beat him senseless with them. Though contrary to the male nature, avoiding conflict with a Mommy is the only intelligent choice.

This choice is based on the military theory of Strategic Retreat. After all, a battle never fought is a battle never lost. Such thinking may offend your machismo, but remember: a Mommy is an overwhelmingly superior opponent.

You'll win a skirmish here and there, but she'll eventually wear you down because a Mommy never quits. She'll re-fight each battle over and over and over, until you surrender. With such a formidable foe, you win simply by not losing.

One of the greatest practitioners of Conflict Avoidance we know has been married to the same woman for 50 years. Fifty years! How has he done it? Conflict Avoidance. In fact, this singular human being has raised Conflict Avoidance to a Zen-like level of sublimity, created a Tao of Conflict Avoidance, if you will. His key tool of avoidance was the newspaper.* If he felt tensions rising, he would avoid confrontation by immersing himself in the newspaper.

Newspapers were all he had.

Not only were there no pro sports teams in the entire state, television didn't even exist for the first few years of his marriage! Imagine married life without ESPN and you'll understand why he has lifetime subscriptions to four newspapers and three weekly news magazines.

It's a testament to the incredible score-keeping power of Mommies that this particular man has become a Conflict Avoider. By instinct he is a warrior. In World War II he flew more than 35 successful B-17 bombing missions over occupied Europe, commanding a lumbering 33-ton, four-engine giant with eleven crewmen through anti-aircraft flak and deadly Luftwaffe fighters. His steely nerves kept the aircraft straight and true, allowing the bombardier the time and stability to make a "good drop." His courage to look death straight in the eye, without blinking, was part of the reason the entire world was saved from the dreaded blitzkrieg and storm troopers of the Nazis.

But a fiery death at the hands of Nazis is one thing, Mommies are quite another.

These days our hero pilot avoids conflict by hiding under his cars. He keeps three of them around, and busies himself with constantly changing their oil in order to keep his Mommy from shooting him down at will.

If you must do battle, we recommend adopting General Douglas MacArthur's famous World War II leap-frog strategy. MacArthur's goal was to secure victory against Japan quickly, with the fewest possible casualties. Had he succumbed to his macho instincts, MacArthur would have pushed straight for Tokyo, taking on the Japanese on their island fortresses across the western Pacific. That would have been a bloody mistake.

Instead, he leap-frogged around the most heavily-fortified bases, attacking behind these main defenses. He then cut off the Japanese supply lines, isolating the island redoubts and effectively neutralizing them.

The rest is history. MacArthur got what he wanted without attacking the powerful and highly-motivated Japanese military head to head. He went around them to get what he wanted. It worked for the General then, it will work for you now!

*The Refuge of Newspapers

Gutenberg took a good shot at it back in the year 1455. His concept was simple: use his new invention to print stuff for the men folk to read at home—thereby creating a pastime for men that required quiet surroundings and concentration. He figured that meddling medieval Mommies wouldn't bother the man of the house while he was reading.

Johann missed the boat by printing the Bible.

Men tried to use the Bible for refuge, but it just didn't work. Mommies wanted to read the Bible *with* them—and *share* their thoughts about it. They even began to form *study groups* to read and discuss Biblical concepts. Something clearly had to change.

It took less than one hundred years for men to come up with a different use of the printing press—THE NEWSPAPER. Our ship had come in.

We all know we should spend more time with our wives and children. But let's face it, sometimes the experience gets a little too rich. Dare we say, claustrophobic? At these moments, most of us would rather slip out the door for the refuge of a local sports bar. While a perfectly understandable response to a concentrated dose of Mommy and the kids, we recommend an old fashioned, tried and true alternative: Stay home and read... **the newspaper.**

Sure, no one subscribes to the damn things anymore, but they worked for our fathers then and can work for us now. Besides, they are more user-friendly and defensible than sitting in front of the computer where you can be accused of such frivolousness as playing a game or surfing the Net.

However lame, the newspaper is an under-utilized but incredibly versatile tool. Follow this advice and extract uninterrupted blocks of solitude whenever you please, in some cases up to three minutes! Here's how it works:

A newspaper's most important properties are its relatively large size and opacity. These features suggest a newspaper's greatest utility, as a shield—lightweight and highly-portable personal armor.

Proper Shielding Technique

1. The newspaper shield is obviously a defensive weapon, suitable for retrenching into positions of seclusion on the domestic front, often right there, surrounded by your entire family! "Reading" in a private study is best, but a big chair in the corner will suffice.

2. Once in your seat, open the paper and hold it up between you and Mommy. This should give her the impression that you are actually reading the paper and it's an important use of your time.

3. The shield maneuver is well known to Mommies-In-Law, and they have told their daughters what to look for. The most common mistake is attempting to totally "hide" behind it.

Use your shield like the gallant knights of King Arthur's court. They never hid completely behind their shield, because they would've taken their eyes off the dangerous fire-breathing dragon.

CHAPTER 5

Learning to Listen

*"A good listener is not only popular with
everyone, but after awhile he knows something."*

—WILSON MIZNER

"My husband never listens
to me" is one of the top three complaints of married women. It
is in the top three because it's true. Most husbands don't listen
because they think Mommies have nothing to say. They are
wrong. Mommies have a lot to say.

Think of listening to Mommy as being on a reconnaissance
mission behind enemy lines. Your goal is to gather information
and clues to what she's thinking and how she's deploying her
strength. Inevitably, she'll give away all sorts of important
information, such as what she wants you to do around the
house, family functions she expects you to attend, or what she
wants for her birthday. If you listen very carefully, she may
even remind you of the actual date of her birth!

We realize that listening intently to a Mommy can be challenging. However, given its importance to your well being, we urge you to try hard, and to be especially alert for the following **Important Words and Phrases:**

my period	my children	your family
my sister's	your garbage	our anniversary
my migraine	your weight	any reference to a household appliance
my car	your snoring	
my mother	your son	any comparison of your financial situation to anyone else
my birthday	your drinking	
my checkbook	your gambling	
my hair	your friends	

Whenever Mommy applies any of these phrases to you, immediately commence the earthquake preparedness drill: **Drop, cover, and hold!**

How To Listen Effectively

When you hear one of the Important Words or Phrases, listen intently for what is said immediately *afterward*. It is here that Mommy will inevitably say something requiring a response or action from you. This is when you are in the greatest danger of idly saying something or reacting in a way you'll regret for weeks, even years.

For example, the standard non-listening male might over-hear the following Mommy-to-Mommy phone conversation:

"And then I said, **Blah Blah Blah Blah,** and she said, **Wah Wah Wah?,** and I said, **Blah Blah Blah,** and you wouldn't believe it **Blah Blah Blah.** Isn't that great?"

Now let's look at the *exact* same statement to see the *hidden* clues that the enlightened male would hear by *listening* for the Important Words and Phrases that the non-listener missed.

"Blah Blah Blah, *on our anniversary I'd like to go away for a few days* , Blah Blah Blah, *when is your anniversary?* Blah Blah Blah, *our anniversary is next Thursday.* "Blah, Blah, Blah *but Mom called and I asked her to take the kids and she said, 'yes.'* Isn't that great?"

Clearly, by listening for Important Key Words and Phrases, our man has armed himself with information. This information gives him the ability to choose between the two standard options for all men married to Mommies:

Option 1: Do nothing

or

Option 2: Buy Mommy a present

While investigating the Important Words and Phrases, we stumbled across a unique group of words that all begin with the letter "I," but spell trouble for you! These words also require the Earthquake Drill!

Immature	Illegal	Impatient
Irresponsible	Impetuous	Inebriated
Inadequate	Impossible	Inappropriate
Insensitive	Incompetent	Immoral
	Infantile	

CHAPTER 6

You Have a Friend in Vagueness

*"The inner condition of the formless is inscrutable,
whereas the condition of those who have adopted
a specific form is obvious. The inscrutable win, the
obvious lose."*

—DU MU (4TH CENTURY CHINESE WARRIOR)

Specificity is the bane of a
married man's existence. It is the enemy, can only do harm, and
must be avoided whenever possible. This axiom applies to all
aspects of marriage—from the minutia to the momentous.
When you are specific about *anything*—what you have done or
will do, where you've been or where you are going, what you
think or what you remember—you've set a clear and well-
defined target in which even the most benign and loving wife
cannot resist shooting holes. Vagueness is always the best
option. It gives a guy room to maneuver, reducing the risk of
being caught in the crosshairs of Mommy's rancor.

Vagueness also helps avoid the tempting trap of an easy lie, of sooner or later painting oneself into the dreaded corner. Lies are hard and angular; vagueness is without substance or sharp edges on which you can accidentally cut yourself. The uniform use of imprecision means less trauma and a calmer marital relationship. This can be attained by building your marriage squarely on the ambiguous foundation of vagueness.

We recommend memorizing the following **List of Vague Terms** and incorporating them into your vocabulary as much as possible.

sounds good	about	thereabouts
I'll try	not too late	not before
a little after	might	the weather
that might be nice	pretty soon	the bridge
around	probably	the traffic
not too long	should	hmmm...

But the most important vague term is actually a single word. "**Soon**" stands alone at the fog enshrouded pinnacle of vague terms. "See you soon" or "I'll be done soon" are wonderfully meaningless phrases that can win you hours of free time.

Think of it: Soon. When is that? It's never! Soon is not a specific point in time. It's an ethereal length of time. Soon can be seconds or even microseconds. For example, "soon" may have been what the Taliban tank commander answered when his driver asked, "When will that American air-to-surface missile destroy our tank?" Or "soon" can mean centuries. "Soon," said the geologist when asked, "When will the San Andreas Fault just give up the ghost and send the entire L.A. basin sailing off into the blue Pacific?"

A word with that amount of latitude is truly your best friend. Like a best friend you can rely on it, visit it often, but never abuse it. Invite this friend into your life, and you will avoid innumerable unnecessary altercations with Mommy. If you do, we guarantee your marriage to Mommy will improve—soon.

From the Mumble to the Cough

There are techniques of vagueness that don't involve words. Throughout the ages the mumble and the grunt have been the backbone of communicating with Mommy. Grunting, as we all know, dates back to the caveman. Mumbling didn't evolve until guys developed more articulate speech capabilities. Gradually, over the ensuing centuries, two higher forms of communication evolved—the wince and the cough.

We know of a guy who is so good with these techniques that he is able to negotiate entire agreements with his wife without ever speaking an intelligible word! He simply mumbles, grunts, winces, and occasionally coughs, forcing his Mommy to play a sort of blindman's bluff until she hits on an acceptable accommodation to him! He then mumbles an affirmative grunt and withdraws to the safety of his newspaper.

Wincing

The *wince* is a tactic used to negotiate with Mommy, without speaking a word.

Correct wincing is always performed with a pained expression while simultaneously breathing in through already clenched teeth. The whistling noise that is caused by the air rushing through your clenched teeth is crucial to the overall impact. For added effect, try hunching your shoulders a bit, creating a constricted, uncomfortable appearance to your body language. Think how Clint Eastwood looked in those old westerns as they pulled a burning arrow out of his leg. Try to capture that tough but distressed expression.

Always complete the wincing communique by exhaling through pursed lips while ever so slightly shaking your head side to side and looking mournfully downward.

With your inhale, you have announced that whatever Mommy has proposed is just "too painful for words." While exhaling, you have communicated two things in succession. First, "I'm trying to work with you on this," and second "I don't really see how this is ever going to happen."

Wincemasters take the wince to a higher level by running their hands through their hair from front to back and finish by rubbing their neck. A good example of this can be seen in those old black-and-white photographs of President Kennedy in the Oval Office after he got the bad news about the Bay of Pigs.

The Cough

The most under-appreciated communication tool is "the cough." Used properly, it can buy the precious commodity of time just when you need it most—when under a full-scale surprise Mommy Moment, with no escape route. We've all been there. It is not unlike the feeling that would overcome you if suddenly thrown off a boat into frigid, storm-tossed seas without a life jacket.

Just as a life preserver tossed at the right moment can give a floundering sailor something to hold onto until help arrives, so the timely use of "the cough" can offer a brief moment to search for a way out of any desperate situation.

The correct cough will break up the cadence of the inquisition, and if you're lucky will distract Mommy to the point that she loses track of her position altogether! Timing is critical.

The length of your coughing spasm should be exactly the length needed to come up with a rational response to the situation you're facing.

Finally, if the predicament is truly desperate you can fall back to the "coughing fit." This is where you cough and gasp and cough and gasp and then in a strained whisper while pointing at your throat say "can't... cough, cough... talk... cough... water"—then you stumble off to get a drink of water. This process can buy up to five minutes, plenty of time to come up with a plausible response. If necessary, you can make it all the way to the back door for some "fresh air." At that point, you could run for it, and, if the situation warrants, call your lawyer.

CHAPTER 7

AAQWAQ
The Art Of Answering A Question With A Question

"Are you talkin' to me?"

—TRAVIS BICKLE

When vagueness fails, salvation lies in AAQWAQ.

AAQWAQ, pronounced "A-QUACK," is fundamental to, and a basic building block of, our underlying philosophy of retreat in the face of Mommy's overwhelming inquisitive power. If marriage were a fencing match, one would use AAQWAQ for the same purpose as a parry; a quick maneuver to gain time and information about the opponent's strategy. Like the parry, AAQWAQ is not totally defensive. It is a verbal riposte which Mommy *must* deal with before she can continue her attack. If she foolishly attempts to ignore your parry, she can easily lose the entire match!

Used properly, an AAQWAQ can abruptly change the topic of a conversation. Since the topic with Mommy is usually *you* and how *you* have screwed up, any change is a good change.

As any field commander will tell you, given enough time and information you can overcome insurmountable odds and win almost any battle. Thus, when faced with a probing question from Mommy—to which a direct and frank response will immediately reduce you to a "bad dog"—pause a moment, maybe two, as you consider your peril. Then calmly answer her with a question of your own. *Voilà!* You have changed the subject (or at least impeded her advance) as you also gain precious *time* to tease out the information you vitally need to survive this Mommy Moment.

AAQWAQ Example

She: "Where were you? I tried to call and they said you'd already left."

He: "Oh? Why were you trying to call? What's up?"

Let's examine what has happened here:

A: They have exchanged words, almost had a conversation! (Mommies love conversations.)

B: Because of his use of AAQWAQs, Mommy has asked and he has responded, but she is no nearer to knowing where he was than before she asked.

C: He's artfully redirected the conversation and is no longer in the "red zone" talking of his whereabouts. Instead, he has slipped into the "green zone" of talking about Mommy and the reason she called!

Helpful List of AAQWAQs
These AAQWAQs can be used whenever Mommy gets you into a tight spot.

Type of Question	AAQWAQ
Location question	
I was there. Where were you?	When were you there?
Time questions	
I called, where were you?	When did you call?
When did you get home?	Kinda late. What time did you go to sleep?
Other women questions	
Were you looking at her?	Have you lost weight?
Were you talking to her?	Have you lost weight?
Appearance questions	
Do you like this dress I bought?	Have you lost weight?
Do you think my butt looks big in these jeans?	Have you lost weight?
Even though I'm in my third trimester, do you think I'm still sexy?	Have you lost weight?

CHAPTER 8

On Being Late

"Punctuality is the thief of time."

—OSCAR WILDE

Have you ever been reamed for coming home "late?" Late for what? Were you going somewhere? Was a bus leaving? Was class starting? Were people coming over? **NO!** Mommies just want you home. They are compelled to control.

Coming home "late" is an evil figment of Mommy's imagination. In fact, the paradox of getting reamed for being late is that *Mommies* are much more likely to actually be late—or *make* you late. For example, have *you* ever lingered before the bathroom mirror so long that you both were late to the movies? Have *you* fussed over packing for a trip so that you missed an airplane? Now *that's* late. You are by contrast an innocent.

Lateness problems can be broken into three categories:

1. The Set Time Mistake

2. The AWOL Mistake

3. The Time of Special Significance

1. The Set Time Mistake

Married men are their own worst enemies when it comes to
the issue of coming home "late." They unwittingly agree to
specific deadlines, which inevitably lead to their failure and
rising tensions on the homefront. This is commonly known as
the **"Set Time Mistake."**

It happens oh so innocently, but oh so quickly. Just as Mr.
Field Mouse going about his daily routine is unaware of the
danger circling above him in the form of Mrs. Hawk, many
guys get up, get ready for work and are already thinking about
what they need to get done that day, when they hear that lilting
question that seems so innocent, loving and pure: "What time
will you be home, honey?" Without thinking, like Mr. Mouse
they walk directly into Mrs. Hawk's talons and mumble "six
o'clock, honey." Then, flushed with formless thoughts vaguely
resembling love, they head off to start their busy work day.

Now they are screwed.

If they arrive any time after 6:03, Mommy will declare
them "late," tensions will rise, and a Mommy Moment of
unpredictable magnitude will erupt. In addition, they have set
themselves up for repeated failure. There are 260 work days a

year. If they're "on time" 90% of the time, they're still *late* once a month. That means every 4th week, Mommy's pissed. Being on-time 90% of the time quickly becomes, "You're *always* late."

Never, under any circumstances, **agree to be home at a specific time.** There is no upside to this. The best you can do is break even.

Far better to simply consult our List of Vague Terms in Chapter 6. Our modifiers give the illusion of specificity, with none of its pitfalls. In the case above, for example, we would have recommended "about" or "around" six o'clock. See how easy that is to say, how harmless it sounds?

She: "When can I expect you?"

He: "Around six, honey."

She: "OK, see you then."

Beautiful! She says, "See you then," and she doesn't even know when *then* is! He's free until 6:59!

We suggest adding, "I can hardly wait" or "I'm looking forward to seeing you" because it furthers the illusion that you are hurrying straight home to see her, rather then "dawdling" over a beer with the guys after work. Adding the AAQWAQ, "What's for dinner?" is also recommended because it diverts attention away from you, and what time you will be home, to her and what she may be doing before you get home.

This same technique can be used when going out with the guys for the evening. Our favorite response to the predictable

"When will you be home?" question is a specific time prefaced with the phrase "not before." Look how well it works:

> She: "When will you be home, honey?"

> He: "WHEW! Hard to say. Probably not before midnight, I'm afraid."

Let's analyze this exchange. She has asked, and he has answered. There's even a specific time of day floating around. But look carefully. He hasn't answered her question!

She's asked when he *will* be home and he's told her when he *won't*. The only commitment he's made is to specifically *not* be home before midnight. One could then say that any time after midnight is fine. 1 A.M.? Sure! That's not before midnight is it? 2 A.M.? Even better! And look at the qualifiers, "Whew!" then "Hard to say" and "I'm afraid." They give the whole response such a wonderful feeling of sincerity, understanding and attempted precision. Don't you love "I'm afraid!?" Afraid of what? It's wonderfully meaningless—and it works!

2. The AWOL Mistake

Another way guys often set themselves up for failure is by making the "Absent Without Leave Mistake." This most often occurs when some buddies or a group of co-workers have an unplanned, after-work function and suck their married-to-Mommy buddy into joining them. He agrees to "just one" and suddenly it's past the time he's expected home. This realization usually occurs just as the waitress has brought another fresh one.

What to do? If he calls now, Mommy will be pissed and ream him out on the phone. Then when he gets home, she'll ream him again. On the other hand, if he doesn't call, she'll only be able to ream him once—when he gets home. So as he begins to sip his fresh drink, he erroneously figures the best option is not calling her. This is a rational decision, however it is also: **The AWOL Mistake.**

You must ensure that AWOL episodes occur only rarely, like visits from Halley's Comet or moments when a sober Mommy suggests oral sex. If you make this mistake more than once in a blue moon you will set Mommy's world akimbo by undermining her trust in you. Mommies are big on trust, as well as schedules, control, predictability in all things, the fundamental goodness of mankind and… speed bumps. You go AWOL and she loses balance. In her mind you not only have acted irresponsibly (oops, an "I" word!), but you've violated the *schedule* and are therefore not to be trusted. Further, by simply vanishing, you've unhappily surprised her (bad dog!) and demonstrated you can go out of control (bad, bad dog!), thus fueling her latent existential horror that the universe really is random. Her world is tilted out of balance, and she must right it the only way she knows—*by reaming you out!*

This earth-shaking, marriage breaking event could have easily been avoided had our theoretical hubby simply stayed alert. If our hubby was like most guys, he would have only considered two options:

> **Option A.** He could have really had just one and gone home.

> Or,

> **Option B.** He could have not joined in the fun at all.

We say, "B.S." to those Mommy-approved options! **GO FOR IT!** Life's too short; aneurysms, lay-offs, and divorce lawyers lie in wait. To start enjoying what life you can, just follow the simple AWOL Solution.

AWOL Solution

1. Be mindful of the time.

2. Be mindful that you are married to Mommy.

3. Approximately 35 minutes *before* the time Mommy expects you home, call her to explain the situation, and that you'll be home "later."

This maneuver will help you avoid the difficulty described above and minimize the damage. Here's why:

A. You are not only calling prior to the time you are due home, you are calling early *enough* that *if* you left for home at that moment, you'd be home when Mommy expected you. She can't ream you for being late, cause you're not late…yet!

B. By calling early, you also have mitigated the shock to Mommy. Now she can *plan* for you not being home. Mommies like to plan. It restores their sense of control and predictability. It calms them.

"Yeah, but," you say, "what if I call and she starts reaming on me anyway and demands that I come home immediately?"

This is a common occurrence and here is the solution for it:

The Magic Houdini Cell Phone Trick

Pretend you're on a malfunctioning cell phone, intermittantly rub the mouthpiece with your shirt sleeve while saying "What? What? You're breaking up. I'll... b... home... later, I... ove... ou." Then hang up and turn off your phone.

---

3. The Time of Special Significance

We would be remiss if we failed to mention one more form of lateness, and this one has "special significance." Even if you have followed all the guidelines about being vague and not committing to a specific time, the unique aspect of this lateness is, if you come home *after midnight,* in Mommy's mind, you're late. No matter what.

Midnight is a **Time Of Special Significance** in the minds of most Mommies. 11:55 fine, 12:05 late! What's more, the later you are after midnight, the worse the consequences.

Why Mommies behave this way has been a mystery until now. Our research has found this special situation of lateness has a unique element not present in other "home late" situations. After midnight, Mommy starts worrying about *you.* That is what makes this a **Time of Special Significance.**

Her anxiety divides itself into three distinct time frames:

1. **THE MIDNIGHT TO 1 a.m. WORRY:** During this period of time, Mommy is worried primarily about your safety.

2. **THE 1 a.m. TO 2 a.m. WORRY**: Her concern now shifts from your well-being to worrying whether you're having entirely too much fun without her.

3. **THE AFTER 2 a.m. WORRY**: Now a new fear creeps into Mommy's mind. Suddenly she suspects that you are having—SEX WITH ANOTHER WOMAN!

Here are the solutions:

1. **THE MIDNIGHT TO 1 a.m. WORRY**: Even if you're sober enough to drive, take a cab. Reasons:

   A. It negates Mommy's "You-can't-stay-out-late-cause-I-think-you're-going-to-drink-and-drive-and-run-into-a-tree" argument.

   B. It shows Mommy what a responsible guy you are. (Mommies love responsibility.)

2. **THE 1 a.m. TO 2 a.m. WORRY**: You're having too much fun without her. This is a tough one. We suggest the following:

   A. Encourage her to go out and have fun with "the girls."

   B. Tell her it was a "different" kind of fun, not like the "real fun" you enjoy with her.

   C. Tell her it wasn't that much fun. That's why you do it only three or four times a month.

3. **THE AFTER 2 a.m. WORRY**: You're having sex with another women. We suggest two alternative approaches:

    A. First, use an AAQWAQ by asking her what's so special about coming home after 2 A.M. She'll say something like: "Well, the bars close at 2 A.M. What do you *do* after 2 A.M.?" Of course, what she's really thinking is: "After the bars close and you're not home, I think you're out having sex with some tramp you picked up at closing time."

        After you've flushed her out on this one, ask her the following question: "If I was going to have sex with another woman, and didn't want you to find out about it, wouldn't it make more sense to do it earlier in the evening and get home on time?"

    B. Tell her even though there's a joke that says, "The girls get prettier at closing time," the ones that are still there at that hour really *are* ugly (not that you ever looked).

CHAPTER 9

Work:
Making It Work for You

"Let us work without protest; it is the only way to make life endurable."

—VOLTAIRE

Husbands work, it's what they do. The symbiotic reasons are simple: Mommy's "keep up with the Joneses" lifestyle costs money to maintain, and work provides the most legitimate escape for men who are married to Mommies.

This wasn't always so. The historical roots of work reach back to the dawn of mankind. Before becoming "hunter-gatherers," our early ancestors were just "gatherers." Men hung around with women "gathering" all day. Even though stronger and faster than the women, men were relegated the same mundane, cud-chewing task. There they were, side by side, all day long... gathering. It must have been stupefying.

Then some prehistoric genius dreamed up the concept of hunting. With hunting, men not only got away from their Cave Mommies and all the boring gathering, but there was also the exciting bonus of running around with sharp objects in their hands!

Men hunted. Mommies gathered. It was such a logical separation of duties. Think about how great it must have been—Mommy-approved hunting trips with the guys two or three times a month. And when they returned from their dangerous outings, the Cave Mommies would screw their eyes out in gratitude for the dinner they brought home! It was a Mesozoic marvel!

This arrangement held together for hundreds of thousands of years, until some fool domesticated a few animals. No more need for hunting; we were growing our own. Farms became the norm and men were domesticated right along with the pigs, cows, and sheep. Farms had it all. Food *and* shelter. Guys were trapped for centuries, working the soil under the watchful eye of their somber, homestead-hardened Mommies.

The experience nearly plowed us under. Then, fortuitously, modern "work" came to be. Originally designed as an easier way to scratch out an existence, work quickly made possible a higher utility: freeing males from house and garden and permitting them to once again hang around with other guys. Finally, they could bring home the bacon without having to raise the pig. Hog heaven!

"Work" wondrously performed these vital functions until...

The Great Undoing!

Work, as an escape for men, reached its zenith in the '50s and '60s.

Then came The Great Undoing of the early '70s, when women entered the work force *en masse*. All hell broke loose.

In a few short years women ruined what had taken men centuries to create and perfect. It was criminal.

To understand how great it was back then, we need look no further than the "Rat Pack." Frank, Dean, and Sammy drinking and smoking and having a good time. Back then, men were men, women were women, and martinis were always doubles.

Let's look at the work world of the fabulous '50s. What a time to be a man, especially at work:

1. The U.S. dominated world business.

2. The only women in the workforce were secretaries and receptionists, mostly single and attractive and young (those were the hiring criteria in the '50s).

3. The three-martini lunch was the norm, and fully tax deductible!

4. You could "get frisky" at company parties without fear of being sued or fired.

5. There were no Mommies at work.

6. Repeat. There were no Mommies at work.

In order to understand the staggering impact of The Great Undoing, compare how a big business decision was made in the Fab '50s vs. how such a deal is done today.

50s Business World

Male President: "Should we do the Anderson deal or not?"

Male VP #1: "It's a tough call."

Male VP #2: "Yeah, tough call."

President: "Whoa, its eleven o'clock already. Let's go to the club for lunch and talk this over. " (Men's club, of course.)

VP #1: (*to his secretary*) "Julie honey, we're going to lunch now. By the way, nice sweater, it shows off your two best assets. Be sure and wear it to the company party next week! We'll be back soon."

While at lunch...

President: "So, how about those Packers."

VP #1: "Lombardi's a genius."

VP #2: "Yeah, a genius."

President: "Would you like tickets to next week's game with the Giants? Check with my girl, she'll give 'em to ya'. By the way, the limo's available if you want it." (All tax deductible!)

President: "Let's have another round of martinis." (Tax deductible!)

VP#1: "Sounds good to me."

VP#2: "Yeah, good."

Later, still at lunch...

President: "Uh-oh, its 2:30. I've got a meeting to go to. Let's wrap this up."

In the cab on the way back to the office...

> President: "So what about the Anderson deal?"
>
> VP #1: "I think it's a go."
>
> VP #2: "Yeah, go."
>
> President: "Good work, Johnson. Nice analysis."

As you can see, the '50s business world was great for guys. The workplace was fun and efficient. Decisions were made and deals cut. Sport talk was OK and sex talk was rampant.

Fast Forward to the "Undone" Business World of Today

> *Woman* President: (*hitting intercom button*) "Phillip, it's 10:56. Are Baker and Carlson here for the 11:00 meeting?"
>
> *Male* Secretary Phillip: "Yes ma'am, they are standing by."
>
> Woman President: "Let's get going then, so we can *stay on schedule*; and remind them to turn off their cell phones during the meeting."

At the meeting...

> Woman President: "Now, what about the Anderson deal?"
>
> Guy #1: "Its a tough call, but Johnson and I have prepared a 30-minute multimedia presentation for your review."

Guy #2: "I can't take the credit, my team did all the hard work. And by the way, I can't say enough good things about Baker and his team."

Woman President: "Its great to see you two have set your male egos aside and created such fantastic teamwork amongst your diverse staffs. Your facilitation of this decision-making process has been exemplary and won't go unnoticed in the team-building and productivity enhancement folders in your personnel files. This should be included in your team's upcoming quarterly review that's scheduled for this coming Saturday at 8:17 A.M."

30 minutes later, after a long, boring presentation...

Woman President: "Let's take a three-minute oxygen replenishment break and stretch a little to freshen our minds before *we* make *our* decision."

During the break...

Guy #1 to Guy #2: "Did you see that outfit with the big points Madonna was wearing at the awards show last night? I didn't know she still wore that kind of stuff. It looked kinda like she had her bra on the outside of her dress."

Woman President: (*interrupting*) "Hey guys, let's be sensitive here. This is an office with both men *and* women. That kind of demeaning talk can easily be interpreted as a violation of Section 7, Paragraph A: Sexual Harassment."

Guy #2: (*jumping in nervously to change the subject*) "Yeah, she's right Carlson, we should keep it to something we can all talk about—like, uh, football! (*turning to include her*) "How about those Packers? Some kind of game, wasn't it?"

Woman President: (*with a blinking look of confusion*) "Yeah, whatever. Let's just get back to work!"

Back in the Boardroom...

Woman President: "That was a good presentation, so what's the recommendation?"

Guy #1: "I say we go for it."

Guy #2: "Yeah, go for it."

Woman President: "Let's not be too hasty here. Before we make a final decision, I'd like to have Human Resources, Risk Management, Information Services, our Community Awareness Group, and the diversity ombudsperson take a look and make recommendations to Karen, the acting Chair of our Executive Council. This may require an environmental impact statement as well, so we better send it through our Environmental Insights Team. Pardon me for a minute while I have Phillip schedule a meeting with the heads of each of those departments."

(*On the intercom*) "Phillip, please get Mary, Molly, Sue, Tana, Christine, Amy, and Jane on my schedule ASAP regarding the Anderson deal."

Woman President: (*to the guys*) "Good work gentlemen. Nice analysis."

Guy #1: "Thanks. Say, it's almost lunch time. Would you like to grab a bite?"

Woman President: "No thanks. I'm going for a power walk and then bringing a tofu and sprout sandwich back so I can eat at my desk. Would you like to join me?"

The Perfect Job

In searching for the perfect job, be advised that it should have as many characteristics of prehistoric hunting as possible. Hunting was the original perfect job. It was a marvelous match for the skills of the caveman *and* allowed relief from his Cave Mommy for days on end!

Listed below are key characteristics for the modern job:

WHAT: Have a job that makes lots of money.

WHY: You always need money. It's like bringing home meat from the hunt. Just like a mastodon was better than a rabbit, more money is better than less.

WHAT: Have a job that requires you to travel every once in a while. You know—trade shows, seminars, stuff like that.

WHY: More opportunities to get some time away and do what you want, sometimes for days! Very much like the hunting parties of yore!

WHAT: Have a job that you can make look "stressful."

WHY: Use the "stress" to get special treatment at home. Hey, it's a jungle out there!

WHAT: Have a job that has few, if any, Mommies involved.

WHY: Duh!

If your job matches the majority of the characteristics listed above you're doing OK. If your current job covers only one or two, quit! Remember your job should work for **you**!!!

How We Came to Be Undone

Women believed that they were creating "equality" for themselves by going to work alongside men. But feminism really was just another one of those conspiracies pulled off in the '60s, '70s, and '80s. The Kennedy assassinations, the Bay of Pigs, Iran-Contra, the Oil Crisis, and Women's Liberation. They're all plots. All of 'em!

It started back in the early '60s, where a thing called "Deficit Spending" came into vogue. The government started to spend money like it was toilet paper and had to find a way to pay all the new bills. Raising taxes had worked in the past, but a better way to bring in more money was needed.

Jack Kennedy discovered it. Instead of raising tax rates on the existing working population, he realized that he needed more working people to tax. Kennedy, who knew a thing or two about women, secretly promoted feminism. Kennedy's operatives spread goofy stories about women being second-class citizens, trapped in their own homes and living as financial slaves to their husbands. BINGO! Women went to work.

Before anyone really noticed, women were at work, hooked on the extra income, and the government budget had quadrupled in size. Mankind's hideout, work, was ruined forever!

This Can Be Summarized by the "Liberation Equation"

"Liberate" women from the bonds of servitude in the home,

so

they can work and earn money,

so

the government can tax their income, and have even more money to spend.

Which would have been fine, but...

the women spent all the money they made on new houses and furnishings, driving up housing costs and the general cost of living equal to the amount of money they earned;

and

they became too tired to do what they used to do,

so

we created daycare centers, and hired housekeepers,

so

we've got latchkey kids and exhausted wives (a new reason for no sex),

so

the only winner is the government.

Which would have been fine, but...

since the kids aren't getting raised properly, the increased tax revenue is spent on prisons and job programs,

so

nobody wins.

CHAPTER 10

Home-o'-phobia

"Everybody is always talking about people breaking into houses... but there are more people who want to break out of them."

—THORTON WILDER

Home ownership is commonly referred to as "The American Dream," but it should really be called "Mommy's Dream." Little girls are taught early-on that they won't be happy-ever-after unless it's in a three-bedroom bungalow with a white picket fence.

While the young boys are outside playing "war," the little girls are inside, playing something called "house." From fairy tales to Hollywood, you need look no further than "Snow White" or "Miracle on 42nd Street" to detect the distinct pattern. Sure Snow got Prince Charming, but did you notice the great castle she got in the deal? Yes, home ownership is a dream for women. For men it's often a nightmare!

Studies show that with a new home, the average monthly cost of married life skyrockets from a doable $1,250.00 (cool car, apartment, food, contraceptives, beer) to well over $5,000.00 (mortgage, SUV, diapers and food for 2.35 kids, garden tools, hanging plants, paint, new flatware, gas for the mower, college savings accounts). Houses are also a catalyst for the Mommy-like behaviors examined in this book. Guys are naturally home-o-phobic, but often powerless against the domestic pressures wrought by Mommies and society in general.

When you eventually come to grips with the fact that you *will* purchase a home, you can apply some creativity to the terms of your surrender.

We offer this chart of features and benefits to consider when making the weighty home-buying decision. Refer to it the next time you find yourself bouncing around the countryside in the back seat of some real estate agent's SUV.

Handy Home-Buying Chart

Feature	Benefit
Wet bar	There will be no question as to whether or not you'll entertain.
	Also no question as to whether or not you'll drink.
Over three bathrooms	See dissertation on "Bathrooms."
Minimum three levels *without* intercom	Mommy is barely audible when she's three floors away.

Feature	Benefit
Master bedroom with fireplace	Heat = sex.
Hot tub	See above.
Excellent heating system	See above.
Fireplace in den	See above.
Fireplace in family room	See above.
Nice kitchen	Hey, a guy's gotta eat.
Workshop	Hideout from Mommy.
Big garage	See above.
Den/office	A Mommy-proof bunker for you to perform important "work" without interruption.
Minimal yard	See Chapter 11.

Furniture Museums

Our Features and Benefits chart makes no mention of formal living or dining rooms. That's because they should be avoided at all costs.

These areas are usually filled with expensive furniture and antiques and end up mentally roped off from the more frequented areas of the house. After the first few months of home ownership, Mommies turn them into a sort of "Furniture Museum," to be used only when "important" company comes

69

over. If carpeted, the museum will have semi-permanent vacuum tracks aligned in a symmetrical pattern allowing Mommy to quickly tell if anyone has trespassed on her sacred ground. In order to avoid becoming a curator yourself, we strongly recommend against anything in your home resembling a formal living or dining room.

The typical cost (calculated below) of the average American Furniture Museum is over $250 per month.

- Average square footage of formal living (14x14) and dining room (10x12) areas = 316 sq. ft.

- Average building/purchase cost per square foot = $72.50

- Cost of space—316 x $72.50 = $22,910.00

- Average furniture expenditure (sofa, Duncan Fife table and chairs, "love seat" [right!], silver flatware) = $12,500.00

- Total cost of museum— $22,910 + $12,500 = $35,410.00

Monthly 30 year mortgage impact at 7.5%=   **$255.10/mo**

Think about it: $250 a month for 30 years, just to store dead people's used furniture!

Bathroom Cautions

Women look at bathrooms and see colors and towels and tile and mirrors and "window treatments."

Men see trouble.

It all started back when the outhouse became the inhouse. All of a sudden there was this little room inside the house with a sink, toilet and bathtub. It seemed so convenient.

But no one fully considered the irreversible harm that the indoor bathroom would do to both the sanctum sanctorum offered by the outhouse, and to the romance in a marriage. Until now.

For example, have you been in your little bathroom shaving and had Mommy come in and sit on the toilet to do her business? Kind of weird, isn't it? Your girlfriend never came into the bathroom when you were dating, did she? You know why? Because it wasn't a very sexy thing to do.

What about the reverse situation? Have you ever found yourself sitting there calmly reading the sports page, doing your business and SHE waltzes in to do her make-up or tell you something "important?" There you sit, with her looming over you, unable to finish the paper, or anything else! So you meekly surrender, relinquishing what minutes earlier was your private retreat, but which is now some kind of feminine day spa. AUGGH!

Can anything be done about this? Perhaps. Depending on your situation there are a few courses of action that may put "privy privacy" back in your marriage:

> **Situation:** You're living in a house or apartment that has one small bathroom.

> **Solution:** None—even though you'll tell your wife to stay out, she won't!

Situation: You're in a place that has two bathrooms.

Solution: None—you'll tell your wife that you have two bathrooms, and she'll still find a reason to join you.

Situation: You're one of the fortunate with three or more bathrooms.

Solution: Sorry—she'll root you out regardless of where you may be hiding. Sadly, there is no escape...

Martha Stewart Syndrome

Homeowning Mommies are very susceptible to an affliction known as Martha Stewart Syndrome (MSS). If your Mommy is fully infected, there is no known treatment. You and your besieged bank account are history.

Study your Mommy's actions carefully over time. Has she been spending too much time flipping through the pages of *House Beautiful* and *Better Homes and Gardens* and others of that ilk? Does she try to catch your attention while reading this propaganda, showing you all the "cute" ideas and color schemes? Has she tried to get you to build a gazebo in the back yard? **BEWARE:** These are the early symptoms of a Mommy caught in the throes of **Martha Stewart Syndrome!** It's a high-grade fever of absurd spending that's sure to drive you yet another step closer to bankruptcy.

Fortunately, guys are immune to the syndrome, for it spreads exclusively from Mommy to Mommy. Here's a list of symptoms for your review. Take note so you can take action before it's too late.

MSS: *Progression of Symptoms*

A. Many infections are contracted by a seemingly innocuous "gift subscription" to one of those glossy shelter magazines. If your Mommy has received notice about a gift subscription coming her way, the only option is to move and leave no forwarding address. GET OUT NOW!

B. Has your bed sprouted pillow shams and dust ruffles? What are those sham things anyway? You already have a pillow case, then they want you to stuff the already covered pillow into a "sham." "Shams" is such an appropriate word. And dust ruffles, what are those for? Isn't Mommy dusting already?

C. Is there more than one dried flower arrangement in your household? How about new slip covers on the furniture? Is your Mommy collecting baskets that aren't used for holding stuff?

E. In its final stages, Martha Stewart Syndrome is almost always lethal—to you. You'll know you're done-for when Mommy just can't handle the stress anymore and asks you to start supervising an interior decorator. Or, when you find your Honey-Do list now includes words and phrases like "demising wall," "exposed aggregate," and "master use permit," forcing you to turn it over to a general contractor.

Ridding Mommy of MSS is impossible. But there is always hope. Hope that progress can be made in containing this agonizing condition. Hope that a cure some day will be found.

We've developed a support group for those of you living with the afflicted. They can't be helped, but maybe it's not too late for you. Visit us at our website to share the grief, pain, and monetary loss with your unfortunate brothers. Our web address: **www.marriedtomommy.com.**

CHAPTER 11

The "Honey-Do" List

"Honey Don't"

—RINGO STARR

Whether a homeowner or not, if you are married to a Mommy you know all about **Honey-Do**, a.k.a. **The List**. You may have struggled with it for years. You are not alone. Men have strived for millennia to complete their Honey-Do Lists only to discover one immutable truth:

NO MATTER HOW MANY TASKS YOU COMPLETE, THE SIZE OF THE HONEY-DO LIST NEVER SHRINKS!

This is, in fact, the universal law of The List. When you finish one task, another miraculously appears to take its place. Armed with this knowledge you will learn to pace yourself and not be concerned with the useless concept of "completion."

Always keep in mind: there are very few items on The List that are truly important to a Mommy. It's just that in her mind there are oh-so-many things that need to be done, and *she* isn't happy unless *you* are doing them.

The trick is to manipulate the Honey-Do List so that the tasks she wants done match the ones *you* really want to do. With this accomplished, you can do what you want, all the while gaining valuable points with Mommy!

We advise constructing a chart. First, list the stuff that interests you alongside her Honey-Do List. Below is a real-life example.

Your List	Her Honey-Do List
Mow the lawn	Mow the lawn
Wash your car	Change light bulbs to a "soft white"
Repair faucet	Air out down comforter
Go to liquor store	Turn the indoor plant
	Shampoo the carpet
	Clean behind refrigerator
	Clean the gutters
	Service leafblower
	Rototill the garden
	Clean fireplace
	Wash her car
	Pressure-wash the driveway
	Hang new drapes
	Install closet organizer
	Stack boxes
	Spread the beauty bark
	Unstack boxes
	Repair the faucet
	Wash the dog

Your List *(continued)* | **Her Honey-Do List** *(continued)*

Wash the windows
Prune the trees
Trim the hedge
Fix garage door opener
Take recycle bins to the station
Paint the house
Fix the vacuum
Flip the mattress
Change the doorknobs
Stomp down the garbage
Dog poop patrol
Change the smoke alarm batteries
New countertop in kitchen
Rake the leaves
Sweep the patio
Scoop out the cat box
Hose out the garbage cans
Hang the new suet ball

Now isolate the items on your list with matches from her Honey-Do list:

Your List
Mow the lawn
Repair the faucet
Wash your car
Go to liquor store

Her Honey-Do List
Mow the lawn
Repair the faucet
Wash her car

Follow the next steps to finish your entire list with absolutely no hassles from Mommy.

First: Mow the lawn—it's number one on both lists.

Second: Quickly hose down Mommy's car leaving you time to thoroughly detail yours.

Third: Start working on Mommy's faucet.

But wait! Your list has one-more-item: the liquor store. To accomplish this important task, we recommend using: **The Veil of Incompetence.**

Simply described, the "veil" is an invisible cloak, which if properly deployed will provide shelter from any Mommy Moment. This is because she will be calmed by the knowledge that, however feebly, you are at least working on a Mommy-approved project.

To envelope yourself in the Veil, simply run into "difficulty." The type of difficulty that requires a trip to the hardware store for "parts." This will give you a chance to evade the harsh glare of Mommy's ever-present spotlight of accountability long enough to make your stop at the liquor store.

This trip also gives you the opportunity to accomplish other things of importance to you. You could have a beer with your bud, hit a bucket of balls, play video games, or, of course, have another beer!

When finally at the hardware store, never get everything you need. In fact, you should save reasons to go to the hardware store the way you conserve any other precious commodity—like the bottle of 18-year-old single malt scotch you just bought for a rainy day. When married to a Mommy, intermittent showers are always in the forecast.

Helpful Hints for Employing the Veil

1. Make a lot of guttural noises and swear once in a while, to show Mommy how hard you are working.

2. If you actually intend to complete a project in a short period of time, do it when Mommy isn't around. This will protect your Veil; she won't learn how easy most projects really are.

3. Measure twice and cut once. This rule, first developed by professional carpenters, has found a home in every weekend toolbox across America. Expert incompetents always measure once and cut twice.

Chores

The Veil can be used for more than project incompetence. It can be used as an umbrella to shield you from the relentless rain of Mommy's household CHORES.

Chores can be differentiated from **Projects** by using our simple two-step test:

1. If completion of a Honey-Do task makes no significant difference to the long-term condition of the household… it's a CHORE.

2. If it takes five minutes or less and has to be done more than two times a week… it's a CHORE.

Be aware that chores carry an exaggerated importance in the minds of Mommies. This phenomenon has never been more clearly demonstrated than in a recent *TIME Magazine* essay written by Journalist/Mommy Margaret Carlson, reaming guys for not doing chores. Addressing the issue, she writes:

> "As for chores, let's define the term. A chore is the thing that has to be done right now or all hell breaks loose. A chore is putting in an extra load of laundry or cleaning up after the kids before you get rec-room Pompeii. It's not installing an antique doorknob, planting tomatoes, or grilling salmon for company, which are fun. "

"All hell breaks loose?" Hardly. "Rec-room Pompeii?" Please! This no-fun, hyperbolic perspective is prevalent in all Mommies, especially when chores are at issue.

Even more disturbing: the overarching Mommy mindset. Look again at the above quoted passage. Ms. Carlson is so caught-up in her self-referential Mommy Moment that she's actually reaming on her husband for doing the tasks that *she* wants *him* to do (her list). We guarantee you, Maggie's husband didn't wake up in the morning with antique doorknobs or planting tomatoes on his list! He is obviously married to a Mommy.

The chore-obsessed Mommy mindset lacks any rational basis, but it is a permanent fixture which must be finessed, here's how:

ChoreBeaters©

ChoreBeaters© were developed in our top secret "Lab of Incompetence" to help all guys. Here's a list of the four most common chores and their corresponding ChoreBeater©.

Chore: LAUNDRY DUTY

ChoreBeater©: Get "a little confused" and throw something red in with all the whites. Unless she's smoking hash every now and then, the resulting tie-dye look won't be a big fashion hit with your Mommy!

Chore: BACKYARD POOP PATROL

ChoreBeater©: Wander in with dog poop on your feet *every* time, until Mommy finally breaks.

Chore: DOING THE DISHES

ChoreBeater©: Alternate between way too much soap in the dishwasher and none at all.

Chore: VACUUMING THE CARPETS

ChoreBeater©: Next time vacuuming is on your list, complain about the suction power of the vacuum cleaner. An incompetent attempt to change the bag in the middle of the living room will require you to rent one of those steam cleaners for the rest of the day, but it will free you of this chore forever.

Be careful with this information. Mommy's belief in your incompetence has been constructed on the strained shoulders of our fathers and their fathers before them. Be subtle with your unfortunate lack of grace and skill and you'll continue to strengthen the fabric of the Veil for future generations of incompetents to enjoy!

CHAPTER 12

Sports

"If people don't wanna come out to the park, nobody's gonna stop 'em."

—YOGI BERRA

Marriages to Mommies involve many battles, usually without clear winners or losers. Like all wars of attrition, the battle line changes but a few insignificant yards after any given skirmish. Energy is expended, salvos fired, losses incurred, but the demilitarized zone of peaceful coexistence that defines a marriage to Mommy changes little. Nonetheless, we soldier on.

But men find true solace only in the triumph of clear resolution. This is where sports come in. Spectator sports provide, if only for a few precious hours, the clarity we need. Games are won or lost, champions crowned, careers made or ruined.

We men watch, our noses pressed up against the hard glass of life. We note with pathetic, wistful hope that professional athletes live in this clearly-defined world yet seldom stay with the same team until death do them part. Sure, they sign contracts—just like we did—but eventually they become "free agents."

It's the stuff of dreams.

There's another reason professional sports exist. They provide a legitimate excuse for guys to escape from Mommies. So become a fan like the other wise men of the world. Pick a sport that suits you well, or mix and match as the situation and time of year warrants! But if you must pick only one, the game we recommend is: **Baseball**.

Baseball is the perfect game for you because:

- It's a game in which you, the fan, are *expected* to drink beer!

- It's a game that doesn't require much attention, so you can just shoot the shit with your buds, if you want.

- Many of the players that are neither giants nor in tip-top shape, making it easy to fantasize that you could play in the bigs too!

- You can take the kids, getting credit from Mommy, all the while drinking beer with your buddies.

- It's a game with no time clock. When you go to a ballgame you can never give Mommy a specific time when you'll return home, because no one really knows when the game will end!

    She: "Just where have you been? I thought you said you were going to the game."

    He: "Well honey, what can I say? The game started out like any other game, but it went extra innings, and before I noticed, it was Thanksgiving!"

Baseball's also great because there are games nearly every night and the season lasts so damn long! There are more total opportunities for "watching the game" than any other sport. Opening day is at the beginning of April and the World Series ends around Halloween. That's seven months! Spring training and the Pan American winter league round out the year.

But maybe you'd like an alternative to baseball. A sport in which you are not merely a spectator but a participant. You might consider **Golf**... Don't. As with most other male-only escapes, Mommies have invaded the game. Remember—they want *all* of you.

The demise of golf as a hideout for men has been swift and devastating. Back in the golden era of golf, most courses were designated Men Only. A crack in the dam called "Ladies' Day" appeared, allowing Mommy's entry to the hallowed grounds for one specified day each week. Out of that fissure has emerged a flood of Mommies. They've continued unabated, to the point where most clubs today now have something called "Mens' Day."

Mommy-less golfing is becoming a pleasant memory. But there's one bastion that has yet to be overrun by Mommies... **Fishing**.

Fishing is great because it has most of the same benefits as baseball. You can B.S. with your buds, there's no time limit, you're expected to drink beer, and if you move from one type of fish to the next, the "season" can last all year!

In many ways, fishing surpasses baseball! With fishing, you can go on outings to get the right gear. There are fishing expos to attend. You can tie flies in the solitude of a Mommy-proof basement bunker. And you definitely need a tricked-out boat!

Our bet is on this being the only sport available to guys that won't be inundated by Mommies. Here's why:

- Fish only bite just before dawn, and always when it rains. Mommies rarely belong to the early bird club and rain gear still has not made the cover of *Glamour* magazine.

- There are no toilets on fishing runabouts. Mommies hate peeing in a can, or worse yet, hanging it over the side. They are, shall we say, anatomically challenged.

- A good fisherman is a "lucky" fisherman. The concept of "luck" enables you to use a number of Mommy-repellant fishing quirks, such as: Wearing the same underwear a few days in a row, donning a hat with endearing profanity as its message, and spraying WD-40 on your hands (if you're out of Bait Balm). All these lucky charms will add to your luck of having a Mommy-free fishing escape.

- You catch 'em, you clean 'em. This old saying was developed by fathers to instill responsibility in their sons. Its secondary purpose was to deter Mommy from fishing. Most Mommies abhor cutting the guts out of wet slimy things.

- Bait your own hook. Putting a hook through a slithering, smelly thing is second from the bottom on Mommy's list of favorite things to do.

- Whack 'em upside the head. Third from the bottom is beating the defenseless fish to death with a miniature Louisville Slugger once he's landed.

Special Fishing Equipment Tip

Whenever you go angling with the guys, be sure to take the camera! **Always** take pictures of the rain, the mud, the dangerous, two-seater, single-prop plane at the airport, the embarrassingly unattractive clothes and stupid hats, the wild bears and cougars that prowl the fishing areas, and "Bud," your semi-toothed guide. **Never** take pictures of the heated, covered boat you fished from, the sumptuous lodge you stayed at, or the twins you happened to have run into at the bar.

The Pain Postulation

We recommend prudence when announcing your sports escape intentions to Mommy. This is because she'll likely make your life a "**LIVING HELL**" between when you announce and when you actually make your escape. That being said, there is a personal choice to be made—to announce early, or to announce late.

Those of you meant to play nose-tackle may prefer to announce early and take the predictable, steady, pounding stream of Mommy's off-tackle punishment until it's time to go. If you are more of a wide-receiver type, you'll wait until late in the game before you attempt your zig-zagging sprint to the goal line, only to suffer Mommy's bone-crushing tackle on the one-yard line. In either case, the extent of the damage will be the same. But take heart, once you've earned your short-term freedom, the bruises heal quickly.

We have researched the concept of **Living Hell** and concluded that it was the penetrating mind of Sir Isaac Newton that formulated the Living Hell Theorem. After a reaming from his Mommy, Sir Isaac went outside to escape and sat down under a tree. That's when the apple dropped on his head and got him to thinking about gravity. It also got him thinking about pain, and more specifically, about Mommy-delivered pain.

Newton's little-known "Pain Postulation" states that no matter when you announce your intent to "go out with the boys," the amount of pain inflicted on you by Mommy is a constant.

By mapping the Pain/Time continuum, Newton clearly proved that the volume and mass of pain inflicted by a Mommy following a guy's announcement of a his intended getaway is exactly the same, regardless of when it's announced. (See chart.)

Newton's Pain Postulation Proven on Mommy Pain Charts

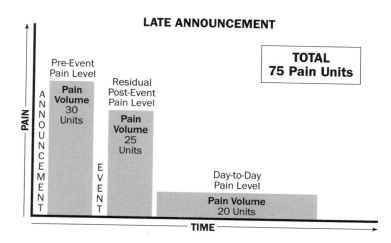

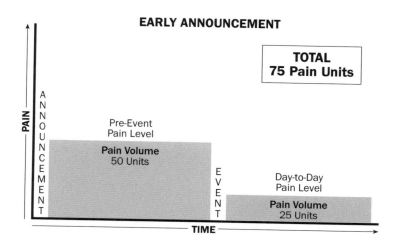

Centuries later, Einstein expanded on Newton's work with the now-famous but often misinterpreted Theory of Momativity, $E=MC^2$, where E=Escape and MC=Mommy's Consternation. Countless scientific experiments have since confirmed the size of Mommy's Consternation is always exponential relative to the size of your Escape.

Einstein realized his new theory would create a field of dark energy in his Mommy. To avoid her inevitable meteor shower of "I" words, he obscured his discovery by dubbing it the "Theory of Relativity," and conjured up that wild story about energy, mass and such. Lucky for him she bought it, even the part about flying a guy in a spaceship faster than the speed of light, returning to Earth younger than when he left! Wow! Einstein truly was a genius.

CHAPTER 13

Cooking for Mommy

*"Offerings of food have been breaking down
barriers for centuries."*

—ESTÉE LAUDER

This chapter isn't about you and Mommy cooking a meal together. Nor is it about a cheap and easy weekend breakfast. This is about *you* cooking an *entire* dinner, all by yourself, for Mommy. You should become the chef in any of the following situations:

A. You're hoping to get laid.

B. She's had to work late for more than 3 days in a row.

C. She hasn't let her Libber flag fly for awhile.

D. You're fed up with her whining about how hard it is to make dinner and you want to show her it isn't all that difficult.

E. You're hoping to get laid.

In order to appreciate the significance of cooking, it's important to understand the deep psychological reason that guys avoid this domestic duty.

It's something so sinister, so dark and powerful, it has never been exposed to the naked light of day. Something so counter-intuitive to men that it's remained a mystery until the printing of this book. The truth is:

You don't cook because
Mommy doesn't want you to!

Oh yeah, she'll act like cooking is a big pain in the ass. She'll make you think that if she never had to cook another meal in her life, it would be like having an endless tea party in the flowering gardens of Windsor Castle with the Queen and the aristocratic ladies of her entourage.

She says she doesn't want to cook, but she does. This is because cooking is a critical part of a recently discovered feminine plot. We call it the "Triple F Conspiracy." It's as shocking as it is logical:

Feed him;

Fuck him; then you can

Forget about him.

Cooking may seem like it's all about serving you. It's not. It's about **POWER**: Mommy's power to keep you around and under her control. Think about it. In the opening stages of marriage there's an abundance of sex. As the marriage matures however, the sex decreases and the man's waistline increases. This is all by design—Mommy's design.

Smart Mommies know that **food** actually comes *before* **sex** on all men's "Hierarchy Of Needs." Armed with this knowledge, the cunning Mommy slowly withdraws sex as she heaps on the Fettucini Alfredo. Eventually, she's able to withdraw the sex completely and just provide the food. Thus the Triple F mutates into a Double F, with you on the receiving end. Double F Mommies accomplish two goals at once:

1. They wean their husbands off the nuisance of sex and onto food.

2. They pork-out their husbands so they won't be as attractive to the husband-thieving Raptor Pre-Mommies lurking in the outside world, thus preserving their own white picket fence, make-a-wish world.

To help you from becoming just another side of beef at the Triple F Ranch, we have developed four complete dinner menus with easy-to-follow recipes—even shopping lists! All of these complete dinners have been thoroughly tested in our Survival Guide Kitchens and are designed to be made start-to-finish in 30 minutes or less, with an absolute minimum of dirty dishes.

Easy Menu #1

Steak a la *your name here*
Caesar Salad
Baked Potato
Carrots au Grand Marnier

Shopping List

1. Get steaks.

2. Get *pre-made* Caesar salad in a bag with the dressing in those little packets.

3. Get 2 Idaho potatoes.

4. Get a bag of pre-peeled baby carrots.

5. Get 2 bottles of red wine (one for you while you cook and one for her and you at dinner).

6. Get 1 pint Haägen Dazs (for her after dinner, while you finish the red wine).

Directions

Step 1: Open wine (to let it "breathe"). Pour yourself a sample.

Step 2: Put spuds in microwave, set on high for10 minutes (*don't start yet*).

Step 3: Open carrot bag, place appropriate amount into steamer pan on stove (*don't start yet*).

Step 4: Tear open salad, shake into individual salad bowls, sprinkle with dressing.

Step 5: Fire up the barbecue.

Step 6: Pour yourself another sample of wine to see how it is developing. Then, without asking if she wants one, pour her a glass and give it to her saying, "Try this. I think it's pretty good. What do you think?"

This can accomplish much. In one simple gesture you:

A. Set the tone that you are serving her (Mommies love to be served).

B. Shown her that you still have a little grace and style (they like that too).

C. Set up a defense against the "Hey, you drank that whole bottle of wine yourself" attack.

D. Softened the time of Mommy's pre-dinner tenseness.

Step 7: Put steaks on BBQ.

Step 8: While steaks are BBQ'ing, push start button on microwave. Turn carrots up to high. Set table.

Step 9: Take steaks off grill, bakers out, carrots in a serving bowl with Grand Marnier Sauce.

Step 10: Serve!

Step 11: Attempt conversation—ask Mommy about her day.

Step 12: Clear table.

Step 13: Serve dessert.

Step 14: Do dishes.

Grand Marnier Sauce Recipe

Shopping List

1. Get a bottle of Grand Marnier.

Directions

Step 1: Pour 2 oz. of Grand Marnier in jigger and set aside on right side of work area.

Step 2: Pick up jigger with right hand and drink in one delicious gulp.

Step 3: Refill jigger with 1 oz. Grand Marnier and drizzle carrots.

Step 4: Repeat Steps 1 and 2 as necessary.

Easy Menu #2

Spaghetti a la Newman and (*your name here*)
Garlic Bread
Caesar Salad
Carrots au Grand Marnier

Shopping List

Same as Easy Menu #1, except:

1. Get "Newman's Own" spaghetti sauce, packaged spaghetti, and pre-made garlic bread in the oven-ready foil bag.

Directions

Same as Easy Menu #1, except:

Step 1: Heat garlic bread in oven.

Step 2: Boil water and throw in noodles (about 10-12 minutes).

Step 3: Drain water off noodles.

Step 4: Put in Newman's Own and smooch around.

Step 5: Open red wine, pour yourself a sample, pour some in spaghetti, and mix.

Step 6: Do salad.

Step 7: Set table.

Step 8: Serve.

Step 9: Converse.

Step 10: Clear table. Serve dessert. Do dishes.

Easy Menu #3

Broached Salmon *à la* (your name here)
Caesar Salad
Baked Potato
Carrots au Grand Marnier

Shopping List

Same as dinner in Easy Menu #1, except:

1. Get **fish**.

Directions

Same as Easy Menu #1.

Easy Menu #4
Special Nite Dinner

Pick any previous menu.

Shopping List

Use appropriate shopping list. **Add candles, a rose in a vase** (with that fern stuff), and **firewood**.

Directions

Prepare as previously noted. Turn down lights, light candles and fire, put rose on table, serve on best china, put more parsley on everything.

There you have it. Four complete dinners designed to make you a culinary champ with a minimum of muss or fuss. The amazing thing about these recipes is that if used sparingly and with a little creative flare, you can rely on them for the entire term of your marriage.

For super extra credit, try these three easy but distinctly different desserts that sound impressive, taste great, but are a "slam dunk" to prepare!

Easy Dessert 1
Cherries Jubilee

Recipe
1. Put vanilla ice cream in a fancy bowl.
2. Pour canned Bing cherries over it.
3. Serve. **Cherries Jubilee! Voilà!**

Easy Dessert 2
Equatorial Ice Cream

Recipe
1. Put vanilla ice cream in a fancy bowl.
2. Pour Kahlua over it.
3. Serve. **Equatorial Ice Cream! Arriba!**

Easy Dessert 3
Kentucky Derby Ice Cream

Recipe
1. Put vanilla ice cream in a fancy bowl.
2. Pour creme de menthe over it.
3. Serve. **Kentucky Derby Ice Cream! Giddy Up!**

Study these dinner and dessert recipes until they become second nature to you. Use them whenever you need to atone for your inevitable screw ups, or loosen the ever-tightening grasp of Mommy's Triple F talons.

CHAPTER 14

Pouching Your Dollars

" The world is his, who has money to go over it. "

—RALPH WALDO EMERSON

"Cash talks, bullshit walks."

—AUTHORS, ET AL.

Financial arguments in any marriage are inevitable, but many can be avoided. This is where the Pouch comes in. Elegant in its simplicity, sublime in its effectiveness, it truly is a marriage saver.

Besides quelling those nagging financial arguments, the Pouch also serves as a tourniquet to stop the bleeding financial wound commonly known as marriage, and redirect some of that hard-earned cash back to you.

Like so many of the concepts in this book, the Pouch has no concrete reality. It's just our metaphor for a separate stockpile of money (always cash), the use of which, *by prior agreement*, is unaccountable to Mommy!

Once established, the proper use of the Pouch will rid your marriage of those trivial financial disagreements forever! Just follow our easy steps.

99

Step 1: Establishing the Pouch Concept

One day over breakfast and out of the blue (dinner will do as well, but never after a fight about money), you announce:

> "I was reading Ann Landers the other day. She was answering a woman who asked how to resolve money disagreements with her spouse. Ann responded with a brilliant suggestion. She recommends *all* couples agree on a dollar amount that *either* spouse can spend without getting prior approval from the other."

The magic of this formula is its apparent fairness. Mommy gets a Pouch, too! This ensures she will agree with the concept. (By the way, this is true! Ann Landers did give birth to the Pouch.)

Step 2: Creating the Pouch Itself

The rules of pouching are simple. Either spouse can, without consulting the other, purchase items costing less than an agreed-upon threshold. The dollar amount, of course, will be different for all of us, depending on our financial situation and Pouch needs. For example, let's say the agreed-upon amount is $50. This means if you see a frivolous little $35 thing-a-ma-bob you've just *got* to have for the car, you could buy it *without* Mommy's prior authorization and not get reamed.

Accountants and the financially astute reader may be thinking, "Great, but how *often* can I buy something? Won't Mommy want to set a limit on the total amount I can spend?" Of course she will—Mommies love limits. Because of this we urge establishing a monthly, rather than quarterly or annual, limit. There are three reasons for this:

1. Monthly limits enable you to scam more spending power with such obfuscations as, "I bought that last month with last month's Pouch."

2. A monthly limit allows you to introduce the concept of the "carry-over." Using this compounding Pouch tool, you carry over "unused" dollars from one accounting period to the next, or as we call it, "Pouching your Pouch."

3. Pouching your Pouch is key to achieving your real goal—Pouch Heaven: the freedom to spend almost any amount of money anytime you want on anything you want! When you have pouched your Pouch to the point of Pouch Heaven, a weekend trip to Vegas with your buddies is within your grasp. When she inevitably questions the expense of the trip you simply say, "Don't worry, honey; it's all out of my Pouch. I've saved it up over the last few months!"

For bigger transactions, you may need to borrow from future Pouch months. The beauty of this technique is that most Mommies have trouble accounting for exactly how many month's worth of Pouch you borrowed. Thus, you can go back to using your Pouch relatively soon, sometimes without skipping a beat!

Step 3: Increasing the Size of Your Pouch

Most Mommies believe they have permanent fishing rights on their husband's income stream. Because of this, you should create as many hidden tributaries as possible ensuring Mommy can't stretch her financial gillnet across all of them all the time. Do this by simply adding cash whenever and wherever possible. **All extra cash goes into the Pouch.**

Tried and True Pouch Builders
Pouch Builder #1: Paychecks, Raises and Bonuses
For most of us, the ever-flowing river of Pouch replenishment lies here. For it is here that you receive a relatively constant stream of dollars out of which you can easily divert small, insignificant amounts for your Pouch. Here are the two basic approaches to workplace compensation:

Paycheck
Never direct deposit your paycheck to the house account! Instead, take it to the bank and extract the appropriate amount of Pouch dollars, deposit the rest into the house account. Don't get greedy. Small amounts regularly added to the Pouch mount up quickly. Consistency is key; never waiver in the amount. Any discrepancy will make a blip on Mommy's financial radar screen.

Raises, Bonuses and Overtime
These opportunities should all be treated with our 75–25 rule of Pouching. Just deposit 75% of the extra dollars in the house account, fatten your Pouch with the remaining 25%.

For example: Say you get a $100 a month raise. Come home all excited and say, "Hey honey, I got a raise. I'll be bringing $75 more home every month! Isn't that great?" Of course it's great. All win-wins are great. In this case, Mommy wins *and* your Pouch wins!

Pouch Builder #2: Quick Cash

- Unless a gift is absolutely perfect or extra special, return it for cash to feed your Pouch. Do this whenever you receive clothes. Return the clothes, Pouch the cash.

- If you get reimbursed for business expenses or mileage, cash the check and Pouch it!

- Put the whole lunch, dinner, or drink tab on your credit card or expense account, and have your buddies reimburse you for their share with pouchable CASH!!

After working on the basics of "Pouching" and crafting your own individual style, you may want to increase the stakes as many Pouch Masters have done.

With years of apprentice study and meditation, a newly ordained Pouch Master we know pouched an entire automobile! He received a car as payment for legal services and keeps the car in a Pouch garage. He drives it around on sunny days, and returns home in his Mommy-approved Ford Taurus.

You may be wondering about Mommy's Pouch. Don't. Most Mommies never build one. Their taut financial gillnet snags all of the loose cash that may float by anyway. The few Mommies that do create a Pouch usually spend their Pouch money on something they think they need around the house, like napkin rings, or more dried flower arrangements.

CHAPTER 15
Imaginary Friends

"She tells him she must go out for the evening, to comfort an old friend who's feeling down."

—THE EAGLES

Understanding the concept of "Pouching" from the previous chapter will help the brazen among us to move on to something a bit more inventive: Imaginary Friends.

The uses of Imaginary Friends vary from situation to situation, but they all boil down to one thing—*preserving your freedom.*

Like the Pouch, an Imaginary Friend is an abstraction. He is a Mommy-approved "friend" that you can go out with:

A. When you think Mommy will ream you if you tell her you're going out with your same old buddies again;
   or,

B. When you'd like to spend time with someone who's not on the Mommy-approved list.

The key to success with your Imaginary Friend is to introduce him early on. In doing so, you'll set a pattern that will become routine as your marriage to Mommy matures. Before you know it, the mere mention of your friend's name will be worth at least an evening of free time. As the years go by you may even be able to create annual out-of-town trips to visit your friend.

There are three basic rules in establishing an Imaginary Friend. *First*, pick a name and a persona. *Second*, create a job for him that Mommy would never understand, and even *you* don't totally understand. Maybe he's a "consultant." It also should be an occupation based out of town, that requires your Imaginary Friend to call on you every so often. *Third*, create an entire relationship with this person.

Imaginary Friends are limited only by your boldness and imagination. Don't overdo it. Your creation must be credible.

A believable Imaginary Friend is challenging. To help, we've sketched one out below.

Standard Issue IF: A Profile

Name: Andy. (Hey, why not? It starts with "A" and it's easy to remember.)

Age: Always five years older than you. This will calm Mommy because being older, Mommy thinks he will have maturity and good judgment.

Marital Status: Married, with two kids: Andy Jr. and Amy. Andy is a "family man."

Wife's Name: April, a safe sounding name that won't threaten Mommy, and it's also easy to remember because it starts with "A."

Wife's Description: You've never met her. (Less information here is better.)

Andy's Occupation: We recommend that Andy be a computer rep. He does business with your company and periodically has to come to town to "integrate your format compatability," "add 3 billion gigabytes to your backside cache," "install 100 baseT," or "dredge your Ethernet port."

While in town "on business," Andy likes to take you out for a drink after work (he pays, negating any budget battles with Mommy), or to "The Game" (he pays again). If lucky, he might invite you to COMDEX, the annual computer show in Las Vegas, where they roll-out next year's models.

Habits: Andy usually has a scotch before dinner. Oh, sometimes he gets confused in the morning and splashes on April's perfume instead of his Old Spice, or grabs her Virginia Slims instead of his Marlboros. Andy can be a little weird, but loveable.

The Funeral

If Mommy starts to snoop around too much, as Mommies all want to do, you can always fabricate your Imaginary Friend's sad, untimely demise.

Be careful not to "do him in" too dramatically. It's best to have the poor guy become ill and take awhile to expire. You may even have to visit him before it's "too late."

Of course, you should go to the funeral if you think you can get away with it! And while you're sad that your friend has passed away, you're not too sad. Just before he died he introduced you to his replacement at work... Bill!

CHAPTER 16

Her Four Special Days

"It's my party and I'll cry if I want to."

—LESLIE GORE

There are four days out of 365 which strike fear in the hearts of all men married to Mommy. They represent less than 2% of the total days in a year, but if you mess up just one, the entire year could be ruined.

Of course we're talking about:

Christmas

Valentine's Day

Her Wedding Anniversary

Her Birthday

Note: *We didn't include Mothers' Day because Mommy is not your Mom. It's worth noting however, that on Mothers' Day, if Mommy doesn't receive a gift from her children, Daddy's in trouble!*

These surely are special days, for they are the days on which the best you can hope for is to break even. If any are mishandled, it can make your marriage a Living Hell for weeks afterward. And it seems when you're nearly recovered from screwing one up, another looms on the horizon. If you screwed up that one last year, Mommy's likely to start the negative vibes weeks before the actual day, reminding you, and all who come near, of your previous failings!

Here's how to handle them in general:

FIRST: *Never* forget you are married to Mommy.

SECOND: *Never* forget the *special* days.

THIRD: *Never* fail to give her some sort of gift on each of the days. It sounds tough, but it's only four gifts a year. Hell, if you stay married 20 years (four times the national average), you'll only have to come up with 80 gifts. With repeatable gifts like flowers, sweaters, and dinner, that works out to maybe 30 or 40 original gifts spread out over 20 years.

We have listed each of the Four Special Days, the most likely screw-ups, and how you can avoid them.

Christmas

Christmas is the easiest because:

A. With all the hoopla starting four months before the Big Day, it's impossible to overlook.

B. Everyone is buying everyone presents. There is a lot of distraction and distraction breeds cover. With cover, this is the Special Day on which she is least likely to be critical of your gift. A guy can, of course, still screw up...

The Piece of Furniture Screw-Up

This one usually begins with Mommy saying something seemingly rational like, "Oh, honey, the new couch we just bought is so expensive, let's just let it be our present to each other this year!" The unenlightened guy will foolishly take a Mommy at her word. The problem becomes uncomfortably apparent on Christmas morning, when he's finished unwrapping the thoughtful little gift she inevitably bought him and finds himself empty handed. It's a painful scene that his score-keeping Mommy will remind him of again and again, months, if not years later.

Solution

Buy Mommy an outfit from Nordstrom. If there isn't a Nordstrom in your town, send away and get the catalogue.
Here's why:

1. Nordstrom always has fashionable clothes so you don't have to worry about staying current with the "new look." Nordstrom does it for you!

2. Mommy *always* needs a new outfit. (In researching for this book we were unable to find a single woman to give us a negative answer to our survey question, "Could you use a new outfit?")

3. Nordstrom has these salespeople they call "Personal Shoppers" who will actually do the shopping for you! All you do is describe your wife, give them her size, favorite style, color, etc. (use your complimentary WIFEGUIDE© provided in this chapter), and they will pick out stuff that fits the criteria you give 'em! It's a no-brainer!

4. Even with all of this support, because you're a guy, you will periodically screw up and get something she hates or is the wrong size. Fear not. Nordstrom to the rescue again. They've got the best return policy in the business!

5. Finally, Nordstrom gifts come in a beautiful box so there's no need to worry about silly, time-consuming gift wrapping.

Use the WIFEGUIDE© and never mess up her Four Special Days again! Fill it out now, clip it out of the book, and put it in your wallet. Refer to it when you get caught with one of those ticklish questions of color, size, or date.

✂

WIFEGUIDE ©	
NAME: PHONE #:	
MAIDEN NAME:	
MOTHER-IN-LAW'S NAME:	
ANNIVERSARY DATE:	**SIZES**
BIRTHDAY:	BRA:
FAVORITES	DRESS*:
FLOWER:	SHOE:
COLOR:	PANTIES*:
FOOD:	WEIGHT*:
NORDSTROM PERSONAL SHOPPER: 1-800-964-1800	FLOWER SHOP PHONE #:
*UPDATE ANNUALLY	

Valentine's Day

V-Day is a peculiar holiday. Overrated by women and under-appreciated by men, it's actually a total fabrication! Think about it. On the first Christmas, Christ was born. On the first 4th of July, our nation was born. On the first Thanksgiving the pilgrims at least had dinner.

So, what happened on the first Valentine's Day? Nothing! Zero! Poof! No wonder we always overlook its importance. But Mommies don't, and, as in all of the problems discussed in this book, there is the rub. Presented here are the most typical screw-ups on Valentine's Day and how you can avoid them.

The Lack Of Planning Screw-Up (a.k.a the 11 P.M. Dinner Reservation Mistake)

The 11 P.M. Dinner Reservation Mistake is by far the most common screw-up on Valentine's Day. The problem is not just that 11 P.M. is too late to eat dinner, nor is it a problem that you won't actually get seated until midnight. The real problem is: Mommy will *know* you made the reservation at the last minute and will view this as further proof that you don't cherish and love her.

Here's how it happens:

Feb. 13th, Morning
A guy reading the sports page catches a glimpse of a heart-shaped object in the "living" section which he is about to discard. A low-wattage light bulb starts to glow in his cerebral cortex. "Hey," he realizes, "tomorrow's Valentine's Day." The bulb brightens as he begins to think, "I suppose we should go out to dinner. I better make reservations later today."

Feb. 13th, Evening
Guy: (*on the phone to a very popular French restaurant*) "Hello, is this Antoine's?"

Maître'd: "Oui, c'est Antoine's."

Guy: "Yeah, I'd like to reserve a table for two tomorrow night, say something around 8 P.M."

114

Maître'd: (*laughing that standard French snicker of superiority*)
"Heh-heh, surely you jest, mon ami! It is, how do you
say, *impossible*. Don't you know it's Valentine's Day, our
busiest day of the year?"

Guy: "Oh, yeah, well, ah, do you have anything at some
other time?"

Maître'd: "I'll check. (*long pause on hold while you are
subjected to obscure classical music*) Oui, you are a
lucky man! I have a cancellation! I can seat you
at 11 P.M.!"

Guy: "Great! I'll take it!"

Now he is screwed.

Valentine's Day is one of the busiest days at all restaurants.
You must book early! Here are three ways to avoid this "lack
of planning" screw up.

1. Make your reservations now! Today!—Seriously!

2. Put it in your computer. Use one of those fancy calendar
   programs.

   OR

3. Tell Mommy how much more romantic you think it is
   to have a candle-lit dinner at home. Suggest that you
   really *never* want to go out on Valentine's Day again.
   It's so crowded and noisy. Not quiet and intimate, like
   home (Mommies are drawn to quietude and intimacy.)

One more thing before we move on to the second most
common Valentine's Day screw up. Some guys think they can
get away with the Feb. 13th "let's beat the crowd" dinner. It's a

nice try, and some Mommies let their husband's think they're getting away with it, but most women feel the same way towards a guy who takes them to Valentine's Day dinner on the 13th as they would to a guy who suggested they go to the Senior Prom a day early. If you actually pull off a beat-the-crowd dinner on the 13th, don't expect a V-Day BJ. There's no such thing on the 13th.

Box Of Candy Screw-Up

The second most common Valentine's Day mistake is the Box of Candy Screw-Up.

Perpetrated on an unwitting male population by Madison Avenue and the mainstream media, far too many of us have tripped up on this one. Oh, how they wax-on about the romantic, sensual qualities of expensive chocolate. We've even seen chocolate referred to as an aphrodisiac! Is it any wonder we fall for this hoax?

So where is the problem?

The problem is that nearly all women start a diet on January 2nd, and Valentine's Day lands on the 45th day of the new year! There she is, barely six weeks into her annual Mommy diet-to-nowhere, and, just as she thinks she's hitting her stride, you saunter in with 15,000 calories of her favorite delight.

You're thinking, "Ain't I grand?" and she's thinking, "What an insensitive jerk!" If you're lucky, Mommy won't slide into her, "You never pay any attention to what I'm doing" rant.

Solution

Never buy a Mommy chocolate or candy of any kind on Valentine's Day! Why risk it? Even if she's not on a diet she'll likely categorize it as just another L.M.B.T.N. (Last-Minute-

Better-Than-Nothing) gift and hate you for it. First, because you don't care enough to put any thought into the gift and, second, even while she's gobbling them down, she'll hate *you* for all the extra weight *she's* gaining.

No, chocolate is far too risky. If you must buy her something, stick with flowers.

The Lack of Flowers Screw-Up

Just as you should *never* buy Mommy chocolates on Valentine's Day, you should *always* buy her flowers. This is especially true if she works. As the Valentine's work day draws to a close, a peculiar phenomenon occurs: Women organize themselves into two groups—the beaming Flower Group and the fuming Non-Flower Group.

To make matters worse, the Non-Flower Group thinks that when the Flower Group talks among themselves, they refer to the Non-Flower Group as "those pathetic, unloved creatures." Believe us guys, you don't ever want to come home to a smoldering Mommy who left the office with the Non-Flower Group. We know of one guy who came home to a fuming non-flower Mommy and compounded the problem by presenting her with a five-pound box of chocolate. He ducked, but was washing little pieces of chocolate and that red gooey stuff out of his hair until St. Patty's Day!

Solution

Always buy her flowers.

Supermarket Flowers Screw-Up

You should always buy her flowers, but *never* bring home those pre-packaged cellophane-wrapped atrocities they sell at supermarket checkout counters (and anyone who thinks throwing in that heart-shaped acrylic balloon will *customize* and *personalize* it needs to go back to Chapter 1).

The problem with supermarket flowers is one of conflicting perceptions. Most guys waltz in with them, seeing themselves as a modern version of Cary Grant. Mommies see a moron who might as well be wearing one of those sandwich-type reader boards inscribed with the following Valentine's Day message:

> "Hi, honey. I know Valentine's Day is the day set aside to celebrate love. I know it happens every Feb. 14th, but I take your love for me and our love for each other for granted. In fact, if it were up to me, I'd pretty much ignore the whole thing. I know you don't feel that way, so I figured I should do something. But, you're feelings mean so little to me, I waited until the very last minute and just grabbed whatever they had left at the checkout stand while I was paying for my six-pack. Happy Valentine's Day! We'll have sex later, won't we?"

Her Wedding Anniversary

Her Wedding Anniversary is the most important of Mommy's Four Special Days. This should make it the easiest for guys to remember. It doesn't.

It's not accurate to say guys forget it altogether. Most have memorized the date and can recall it, or come close enough when necessary. The problem again is timing. We remember it, but remember it too late. This is often caused by guys repressing the date because they are stuck in stage two of marital grief: DENIAL.

Then we scramble around trying to come from behind and end up wearing that silly sandwich board again. One of the most common mistakes on this day is:

The 3rd Class Motel Getaway Weekend Screw-Up

Waking up on Wednesday to the fact that your anniversary's on Friday, in a slight panic, you grasp at the idea of a getaway weekend at that romantic little resort you've both talked about. A quick call and, surprise, they're booked solid. This weekend and next! You try getaway resort #2 with the same result. Terrified, you run headlong into the BIG MISTAKE: "Hey," you think, "we don't have to be in the main lodge, we can be in that little motel nearby. We'll have dinner in the lodge anyway, and it'll be cheaper!" Wonder of wonders, that little motel has a vacancy. You make the reservation and slip into the idiot suit—again.

The Fool-Proof Anniversary Solution

Fear not! We told you we wouldn't let you down. We have come up with a fool-proof solution. One which will ensure you *never* forget your anniversary again!

All guys, rich or poor, blue- or white-collar, put on their own socks. Think about it, it's one of the few things we all have in common. So, how can we use this fact to avoid the Big Mistake on this special day? Simple. Go downtown to a tattoo parlor and have them tattoo the date that is *20 days prior* to your actual anniversary date on the top of your left foot.

Then, on the top of your right foot, have them tattoo a call to action, something pithy like, "Make reservations today!"

Then, as you're putting on your socks everyday, read the date on top of your left foot and compare it to the current date on the calendar. When the date on your left foot matches the current date, read the message on the top of your right foot, and bingo! You spring into action with just the right amount of lead time to do something nice for Mommy! It's simple, it's fool proof and it works. We know, we got our tattoos years ago!

The Infamous "Victoria's Secret" Mistake

Of all anniversary mistakes, this one is probably the biggest downer for a guy. That's because, simply put, it can confirm how much of a Mommy he married!

Here's how it happens: A guy probes the deep recesses of his testosterone-soaked mind, trying to come up with something great to get his wife for Her Wedding Anniversary. Sooner or later, like all of us, he hits on what he thinks is a terrific idea—a little sexy something from Victoria's Secret! Maybe something skimpy or lacy or see-through or (dare we think it) **RED!**

As he excitedly digs himself deeper and deeper into this mistake, he's patting himself on the back because this great idea kills two birds with one stone. He's getting her a great present, which she's gonna love, *and* it'll get her into something provocative that will increase his chance of sex! Wrong on both counts.

120

Our surveys show that only 10% of all Mommies who receive anniversary gifts from Victoria's Secret ever wear them. Only 2% even try them on in front of their husbands. This is because:

A. It was probably the wrong size (too small) so they think they look like a big fat cow.

B. Mommies think most stuff from Victoria's Secret makes them look like a hooker.

Solution

Steer clear of Victoria's Secret and stick with the Personal Shoppers at Nordstrom.

Her Birthday

This is a dangerous and confusing day because it's importance changes as the years go by. We all love a little recognition, but some birthdays, depending on Mommy's age, are better played down. Along with being alert to those portentious birthdays, there are classic pitfalls to avoid.

The "Anywhere You Want" Screw-Up

This one usually begins by either completely forgetting Mommy's birthday or, at a minimum, forgetting to do anything about it. Most guys hum along, doing nothing, as Mommy's birthday looms dangerously closer. Usually a day or two before her birthday, when her curiosity bubble bursts, she breaks down and asks what he's planning. Caught off-guard, and not having read this book, he responds substantively with,

"I thought it would be fun to go out for a nice dinner!" Mommy responds with, "Sounds great! Where are we going?" And he answers, smugly, with four innocuous little words that seem harmless, but seal his doom, "**Anywhere you want, honey!**"

Here's the problem. He thinks he's communicating that:

A. He's a big spender and will spare no expense.

B. He'll defer to her choice of restaurants on her big day.

If Mommy thought that way, there would be no problem. But she doesn't. With the words "anywhere you want," Mommy sees him slipping on the sandwich board suit again that reads:

> "I haven't spent any time thinking about you or your birthday, and I don't care enough about you to make the effort to think up a nice thoughtful gift, so I just scrambled and said we'd go out to dinner, figuring that was better than nothing. Furthermore, you matter so little to me that I didn't bother thinking of a cool place we could go, nor did I trouble myself to make reservations. But we'll have sex when we get home from wherever we go, won't we?"

Guys have been digging themselves into holes with this one for years, and not just with birthday dinners. That same four-word phrase will sink you just as fast when used for vacation gifts: "Anywhere you want, honey." Oops! Or getaway hotel overnights, "Anywhere you want, honey." Ouch!

The Quid Pro Quo Screw-Up

Also committed on anniversaries and Valentine's Day, the Quid Pro Quo (QPQ) Screw-Up is simply the result of unreal expectations.

The QPQ Screw-Up occurs when you assume that by giving her something she wants, like a birthday gift, (the QUID) she, in return, will give you something you want, like sex (the QUO).

The downside of this screw-up is relatively minor because when married to a Mommy, a QPQ is just wishful thinking. No harm, no foul.

The downside becomes significantly larger, however, if Mommy realizes you believe you *deserve* a "Quo." Then Mommy will know the only reason you got her the nicely wrapped Quid was to get her Quo. She will assume you were not thinking of her on her big day, but instead were thinking of yourself and your BIG PAL! It all goes downhill from there. A lose-lose.

Far better to just give the present with no expectation of a "Quo," then review the chapter on sex and how to get more of it.

Diamonds...

Finally, a word about a peculiar gift that's appropriate for any of the Special Days—diamonds. What is it about diamonds that sends Mommies into such a flurry of excited showing and telling? The truth about diamonds isn't nearly as pretty as all those bangles and baubles men have been buying women over the centuries.

The ugly truth is:

MOMMIES THINK THE ONE WITH THE MOST DIAMONDS HAS THE MOST POWER

More is good, but bigger is even better! Have you heard of any woman ever returning a diamond because it's too big? Imagine the conversation if it were to happen: "Thank you, honey, but it's just too big. I think I need to exchange it for something smaller, something all my girlfriends will have to squint to see." But the more-and-bigger power game only works if… they are real.

Nothing brings this reality home more clearly than The Question. The Question that sends alarm bells a-ringing in guys' ears: "**Are they *real*?**" It has a knee-shaking resonance to it, doesn't it?

The irony is that many Mommies are perfectly capable of buying off-brand cereal for their children. Mommies will even buy knock-off designer clothing for themselves. But receive fake diamonds as a gift? *Never!* When it comes to diamonds it's not the thought that counts, it's the cost.

Jewelers have promoted this charade for years. Color, cut, and clarity are the watchwords when it comes to purchasing diamonds. Oh, come on! With 21st-century technology, fake diamonds can be manufactured that rival the best of the real stuff. The only way to judge the purity of the stones is with the trained eye of the jeweler himself. Even then, this only happens under bright lights, using one of those fancy microscope eye-pieces. Of course, the simplest way to certify the authenticity and value of those shiny rocks is with the receipt.

DECEPTION PASS: A Solution?

We know of one brave man who may have found a route through the rugged barrier of authenticity. We call him "Marco Polo" because he was the first guy we know to travel this very dangerous path in search of better trade.

"Marco," a CPA no less, happens to have a very good contact in the retail jewelry business. What he does takes guts, but it pays off well for him.

He purchases the simulated stuff with cash, from his Pouch, then takes it to his contact. The contact produces a counterfeit receipt detailing some appropriately absurd amount of money based on what the "real" stuff would cost. A few days before presenting the gift, he leaves the receipt "hidden," where he's sure his compulsively snoopy Mommy will find it! This pre-empts The Question. Confident they are "real," she wears the rocks proudly, parading around town, while winning competition after competition with the other Mommies.

At first we thought there was substantial risk in this scam that our friend hadn't considered. What if Mommy got caught at the jewelry store trying to exchange the phony diamond for an even bigger one? There's a chance she'd be put in handcuffs, hauled off in a squad car, and thrown in jail!

On second thought, maybe there is more here than meets the eye...

CHAPTER 17
Fire and Sex

*"Your words say quit, but I know you're a liar,
'cause when we kiss, mmmm... FIRE!"*

—THE BOSS

"I'm a hunk-a-hunk of burning love."

—THE KING

What's the big deal about hot tubs? Why do young couples vacation on tropical islands? What's so romantic about a fireplace in the bedroom?

The answer to all of these questions is the same. Heat and sex are inter-related. When guys say a woman is "HOT," they mean she is sexy. When they say she is sexy, they mean she is "HOT."

There's a scientific reason for this: Women are wired to reproduce. As a basic requirement of reproduction, women ovulate once a month. When they do, their basal temperature rises slightly. An increased basal temperature sends hormonal signals that trigger their instinctual, overpowering, unstoppable, and all-consuming reproductive drive. When Mommy reaches this point, she is completely overwhelmed by her hormones. Powerless, and lacking her normal indifference to sex, she may begin to think about considering the *concept* of having sex with you.

Therefore: IF YOU WANT TO HAVE SEX WITH A WOMAN, HEAT HER UP.

1. As she warms up, her basal trigger will be tripped.

2. She'll think she's ovulating.

3. She'll be more likely to have sex with you!

Could you imagine where the human race would be if reproduction didn't have a system like this built into it? Without women's temperature-sensitive fertility system, the human family tree would have died while still a sapling. Homo Erectus would have evolved into Homo Flaccidus, extinct before we even got started.

Imagine a caveman trying to get a little:

Caveman: "Let's do the feel-good thing!"

Cavewoman: "Why?"

Fortunately, the caveman had his wits about him and made a warm fur coat for his cave woman. This simple act saved mankind from extinction. But the Earth's population didn't really take off until the caveman discovered fire! This is clearly demonstrated by the following chart.

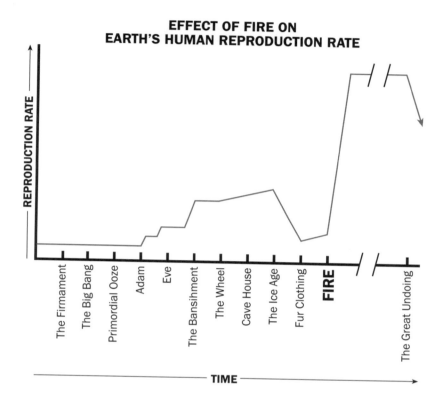

EFFECT OF FIRE ON EARTH'S HUMAN REPRODUCTION RATE

REPRODUCTION RATE

The Firmament
The Big Bang
Primordial Ooze
Adam
Eve
The Bansihment
The Wheel
Cave House
The Ice Age
Fur Clothing
FIRE
The Great Undoing

TIME

CHAPTER 18

The Eleven Types of Married Sex

"The price is exorbitant, the pleasure is transitory, and the position is ridiculous."

—LORD CHESTERFIELD

"I've tried several varieties of sex. The conventional positions make me claustrophobic. And the others give me either a stiff neck or lockjaw."

—TALLULAH BANKHEAD

You don't need Professors of Matrimony to tell you why you like sex so much. This book is dedicated to what's important, and in this case it's that... **YOU WANT MORE!**

In order to get more, you need an intimate understanding of the eleven major types of sex you'll get when married to a Mommy.

The Eleven Types of Married Sex

Type 1: She Initiates

Type 2. You Initiate

Type 3: Vanishing

Type 4. Barter System

Type 5. Controlling

Type 6. Commemorative

Type 7. Charity

Type 8. Obligatory

Type 9. Haircut

Type 10. Trip

Type 11. No

If a guy's been married to a Mommy for more than five years, it's likely that he's been exposed to most of the eleven sex types, even though he may not have been aware of them at the time. We've provided more detail of the eleven sex types in order for you to gain a better perspective, sharpen your skills, and most importantly, **GET MORE!**

Type 1: She Initiates
This is by far the rarest and most coveted type. In fact, if those married to Mommy would ask themselves when the last time their Mommy made a sober sexual advance toward them, they might, after reading this chapter, be forced to answer... "Never!"

It's not that a drunken advance doesn't count—we'll all take them. It's just the anguished despair forced upon you when you realize Mommy only wants to hide the salami when she's smashed!

On average, a guy married to Mommy can expect to get sober Type 1 sex 3.5 times for every ten years of marriage.

To actually experience this rarity, you need to be sensitive to the initiating signals she may send. Often it's just the slightest glance or touch. One guy we know has learned that a soft pat on the elbow when they're in bed is his wife's signal. As we have said throughout this book, you must stay ever vigilant!

Yet we wonder if he's truly getting Type 1 loving. Even a strong signal—like, "C'mere big boy, I'm hot. Take me now!"—doesn't necessarily qualify as Type 1. It could simply be one of the other ten types.

Type 2: You Initiate... and She Does Not Refuse
This is the most common form of married sex.

There are however, a wide range of responses to a husband's Type 2 advances, from what we call "Cocktail Sex" to something we refer to as "Dinner Sex."

Cocktail Sex is desirable Type 2 sex. We compare it to asking your wife if she'd like a drink, and having her respond, "Great idea. In fact, make it a double!"

Dinner Sex, on the other hand is comparable to going out to dinner and asking, "What are you going to have?" and having Mommy respond, "I'm not really hungry, but you go ahead."

Type 3: Vanishing
Blow jobs...

Type 4: Barter System Sex
Often confused with Type 1, this is also known as "Pay-Off Sex." Most guys hate to admit it, but this is often the only sex they get! Type 4 sex takes many forms but they all boil down to the same thing: *you* get sex when *she* gets what she wants!

Type 4 is easily spotted if you keep your wits about you. The next time she comes on to you, try to answer these critical questions:

1. What does she want?

2. Have I given her anything lately?

If you find quick answers to either of the above questions, before you have a sexual blackout, you're the proud recipient of Type 4 sex. Some guys actually like Type 4, because it's so predictable and businesslike.

Type 5: Controlling Sex
Type 5 sex is quite similar to Barter System Sex, but it's not about material things. It's about control. Type 5 sex is used by Mommies who have a thorough understanding of male physiology. These women have learned that there is a finite amount of blood in the human male, and simply put, it can't be in two places at once! This is a form of brainwashing that focuses on your other head.

By keeping most of a guy's blood below the beltline, Type 5 Mommies impair his ability to think non Mommy-approved thoughts. Thoughts like "Boy that secretary looked good today," or "Today's the day I'll go out and buy that hot sports car that I've always wanted," or "What Happened?"

Warning Signs of Type 5 Sex Exposure

Are you or any of your buddies under the influence of Type 5 sex? Here's how to tell:

A. If this chapter makes no sense to you, and you think you have a great sexual relationship with Mommy, and she just *loves* to give you B.J.'s, you are definitely under Type 5 influence. Proceed with extreme caution.

B. You can tell if any of your friends are caught in the tight grip of Type 5 sex by the dazed look in their eyes and the shallow, soft, compliant tenor in their voice. Some may even resemble the actors in the movie "Invasion Of The Body Snatchers."

C. You are definitely infected by Type 5 sex if you willingly go shopping at the mall with Mommy for more than 14 total minutes a year!

Type 6: Commemorative Sex

Commemorative sex is the kind you get reliably on the same sanctioned days, year after year.

Early on in your marriage you won't be too critical of Type 6 episodes. You'll even look forward to them for a while. But time will take its inevitable toll, and sooner or later you'll loath the dependability of it all—Valentine's Day, Anniversary, Birthday, New Year's Eve... and so it goes. You'll learn to dread the total lack of spontaneity, passion, sexual tension, and surprise associated with fulfilling Type 6 obligations. But, knowing that there's no such thing as bad sex, you'll take it anyway.

Type 7: Charity Sex

Often initiated by Mommy, Type 7 sex has been traced to prehistory. When men came back after a long hunt that yielded no results, the women would screw them anyway, because they felt sorry for them. The same holds true in our modern world. If Mommy feels that you've had a bad month she'll give you a little sexual pick-me-up.

Charity Sex is, in some ways, the most lamentable form of sex. It arises more from guilt and pity than emotional passion or even physical desire.

Type 8: Obligatory Sex

During the "don't ask, don't tell" period of the '40s and '50s, Obligatory Sex meant Mommy was fulfilling her conjugal duties every Saturday morning. It was something she just *did*, like clockwork, and didn't talk to the other Mommies about.

The nature of Obligatory Sex experienced a change during the sexual revolution of the '60s and '70s. Suddenly, sex came out of the quietude of the bedroom and was splashed across the cover of every women's magazine with intimidating headlines like, "His G-Spot—Have You Found It Yet?" and "The Big 'O' in 60 Seconds—Yes, Yes, YES!" Inside, Mommies were assaulted by pages packed with stats about orgasm intensity and sexual frequency, along with graphic displays of contorted *Kama Sutra* positions only a double-jointed magician's assistant could pull off!

This heightened awareness of other women's sexual habits has made current-day Mommies increasingly paranoid about their own sexual inadequacies, and is the basis for the shift in the meaning of Obligatory Sex.

Today, the obligation Mommy is fulfilling relates more to her needs than yours. In the 21st Century, Obligatory sex is the kind you get when Mommy thinks it's been an embarrassingly long time since she's had sex with you. Mommy is obliged to have sex not to satisfy you or even fulfill her sexual needs. Mommy is obliged to have sex with you to maintain her delusion that she is holding her own in the competitive "Cosmo" world of women who purport to actually have sex lives.

Obligatory Sex is also driven by Mommy's latent fears that she actually *is* frigid and could get along just fine without it.

Type 9: Haircut Sex

Type 9 sex is known as "Haircut Sex" because like a haircut, you know you should do it, it's kind of a hassle, you know you'll feel better afterward, but left on its own it'll never happen—so you schedule it.

One form of Haircut Sex is commonly recommended in magazines like *Redbook* or *Woman's Day*, where there is often a feature article, titled, "SPICE UP YOUR MARRIAGE: EVEN WITH YOUR BUSY LIFESTYLE." This is when you and she negotiate the date and time to go through the motions.

The second form of Type 9 sex is inked into the schedule by Mommy when she is intent on becoming a Mother. Crudely known as the "Functional Fuck," it is the medical equivalent of taking your prescription medicine, and only slightly more pleasant.

A Mommy intent on motherhood will have read the articles, calculated the percentages, consulted with all her friends, and checked the astrological charts before she begins her procreative campaign. This is lunch-time sex that ain't no "nooner." The sex when a headstand is performed immediately following the act, rather than during it. This is the only sex that hard-core Mommies truly enjoy because it is scheduled, they are creating a baby, and in most cases, it's quickly over with.

Type 10: Trip Sex

Trip Sex is not the type of sex you get on a weekend getaway with Mommy. It's the type you get *before* you leave on a trip without her.

A kissin' cousin of Controlling Sex and a kind of phony Type 1, Trip Sex is physically thrust upon you by a Mommy intent on leaving you sexually spent while away from home, in an attempt to decrease the chances that your libido will get the better of you.

As predictable as Big Ben striking 12, this is the type of sex you can put in your daytimer at the same time as you make your plane reservations. While it does carry with it some demeaning undercurrents, it nevertheless is still sex.

Type 11: No

Those who are truly "Married to Mommy" already know way more than they need to about this one! This is the type you get when you come on to her and she says "let's *cuddle*." She wants you to hold *her* and you want her to hold *it*.

You end up just holding her.

Getting More

Research shows you can increase Type 1 contacts from 3.5 to 6.2 times over a ten-year period by paying close attention to your Mommy at all times and staying in top physical shape. Unfortunately, paying close attention to Mommy over extended periods and keeping in good shape involve both pain and effort.

Drop your foolish quest for the ever-elusive Type 1 sex. All that work for 2.7 additional episodes of Type 1 sex over ten years figures out to only .27 episodes per year. What form would that .27 take anyway? Probably just a little dirty talking, and you can get that on network TV after 8 P.M.!

Alternatively, you can get an abundance of Type 10 Trip Sex by relying on its predictability, and following our simple four-step FAK-A-TRIP© plan, outlined below.

FAK-A-TRIP©

Step 1: Tell Mommy you have to go on a trip for a few days and "schedule" it.

Step 2: Wait for the inevitable.

Step 3: Savor and enjoy.

Step 4: Inform Mommy that the trip has been cancelled* at the last minute.

Helpful Tip: Instead of actually "cancelling" the trip you can "reschedule" it, thereby getting multiple Trip Sex attacks out of the same faux trip!

A Brighter Future

"I can resist everything except temptation."

—OSCAR WILDE

What will you do with all the free time you've gained by practicing the lessons in this book? What will you do with all that additional money you've pouched? What will you do?

Perhaps an affair!

You could join the legions of men who've gotten a little "on the side." It's probably crossed your mind once, or twice. BEWARE: Affairs are costly, complicated, dangerous, and lead to even more expense... divorce.

Besides, those sexy young gazelles that leave you breathless, muttering private indecencies, may seem to be free-spirited nymphs, but they're not! Deep down they are **dormant Mommies**, hoping for a chance to erupt—all over you. Once they do, you're back in the same scalding lava you thought you'd escaped. Don't blame them for deceiving us, they can't help it. Just like we can't stop our reaction to their seductive powers. Guys are often like the stupid little hamster running frantically in his wheel to nowhere. See woman, get trapped, see new woman, dump first woman, get trapped by new woman, get trapped again, and again, and again.

It's true! 95% of all women who become involved in affairs will take guys to the exact same place—MARRIED TO MOMMY! Sadly, there is no escape. Before the printing of this book, the only options have been to trudge along in quiet desperation until your chest explodes and Mommy sells your stuff and moves to the sun belt; or, on the way to an "American Beauty" meltdown, throw open your window of discontent, and scream to all within earshot: "I'm mad as hell and I'm not going to take it anymore!"

Is There a Better Way?

There must be. There has to be.

Of course, by employing this book's philosophies and teachings, the 21st-century " 'til death do us part" marriage will become vastly more livable. But we believe, at the beginning of the third millennium, marriage itself can be improved.

We propose a better way. A way that will transform the current marathon of marriage into an invigorating run for the roses. We propose bold new legislation which would require an automatic "Sunset Clause" be built into every marriage contract. Government-sponsored "wife insurance" if you will.

This simple piece of legislation will require that all marriages last for exactly three years (1095 days)—*and not one day more*. At the end of the first term of marriage, both parties would be automatically and legally "unencumbered," and would have to remain apart for at least six months. After six months in neutral corners, they could, if both parties agree, re-marry and begin another three-year term.

No more trouble with commitment, imagine how much easier it would be standing at the altar:

> **Preacher:** "Do you, John, take this woman, to have and to hold, for better or worse, in sickness and in health, for richer or poorer, forsaking all others, 'til death do you part, or for thirty six months, whichever is sooner?"
>
> **John:** "Sure!"

Knowing it would all be over in 36 months, both parties would work harder to make their marriage fun each and every day. Each spouse would be hard-pressed to feel trapped with freedom just a few pages on the calendar away. The divorce rate would plunge to zero!

There are hidden health benefits as well. At the end of three years, both spouses would be "on the market" again, making it important to present themselves to potential future partners in the best light. The three-year term will happily mark the end of beer-bellied husbands or wives with thighs of large curd cottage cheese.

The zero population growth movement will hail these minimalist marriages as a stroke of genius! A contracted couple would think long and hard before embarking on the road to progeny. Staring the potential of single parenthood straight in the eye should make even the most kiddy-obsessed Mommy blink.

Environmentalists will cheer a decreased average family size because it brings a decrease in consumption, and waste. Far fewer disposable diapers fouling our overburdened landfills!

Our proposal also includes sweeping legislation that will rewrite the tax code while at the same time solve the Social Security mess. We propose eliminating the Social Security tax altogether, and replacing it with a tax equal to 50% of every working man's income.

The "Freedom Tax" will be collected by the Feds and then distributed to each and every woman in the nation. This ensures that women maintain one of the key benefits found in today's long term marriage contract—Financial Security. With this critical piece in place, women will no longer worry about the "S" word; it will come as a birth right. Men, on the other hand, will never suffer the anxiety associated with being captured by a security-hungry pre-Mommy. "Accidental" pregnancies will be a distant memory. Episodes of Type 1 sex will skyrocket! Men will be judged by their charm and character, not their cash flow!

At first, some might think the 50% tax is too much. But if you think about it, guys give 50% away the instant they say, "I Do" (that's why the bride is blushing), and sixty percent when they get divorced. We say what the hell, if you're gonna get financially reamed one way or the other, you might as well give it to them up front and be done with it!

All told, the three-year plan solves the healthcare crises, erases divorce, eliminates the need for marriage counseling, ends overpopulation, stops world hunger, cleans up the environment, eliminates falsehoods in dating relationships, frees women of financial bondage forever, and solves the Social Security dilemma. Most importantly, the uptight, score keeping, back-yard competing, perpetually practical, fear-based, energy depleting, exasperating Mommy mindset would be a thing of the past, thrown out by the new marriage paradigm.

A change like this can't take place without a good old grass roots campaign. To help in the effort, we've included two handy, tear-out letters to fill in and send to your representatives in Washington, D.C. Please note that each letter is specific to the recipient and has been carefully composed to appeal to either a female or male member of congress. *Note the differences and be sure not to mix them up!*

Governmental activism is fun, and this book has made it easier than ever! Simply pick your representative, sign, tear, and send.

MARRIED TO MOMMY?

Congresswoman _____
US House of Representatives
Washington, DC.

Dear Congresswoman,

I, along with millions of my voting sisters, would like you to support term limits. No, not those term limits. Term limits on the currently onerous length of today's marriages.

You see, back when marriage was invented life was difficult, brutish, and short. With a life expectancy of under 30 years, any marriage commitment would last a mere 15 to 20 years. If a woman were especially lucky, the man would die in a hunting accident a few years into the marriage, after the children arrived. The woman could then run out the rest of her days, in the vaulted position of Village Matriarch surrounded by her loving children. Unfortunately, with all the advances in civilization and medicine, a man's average life expectancy has climbed to a stratospheric 77 years!

With the increase of life span has come an unnatural increase in marriage span—it's not uncommon for some marriages to drag on into the 40-, 50-, and 60-year marks. Think of it… sixty years staring across the burnt toast on the breakfast table at the same man, being ignored 90% of the time (unless you are talking about how great he is), smelling his stale farts, listening to the same stupid jokes, pinching the same pennies, watching each other deteriorate into brittle-boned, age-spotted, assisted-living wretches. It's enough to get you to make an appointment with Dr. Kervorkian!

Contrast that with the ability to choose a new man every three years! New romance, new conversations, new experiences, new friends. Never-ending spring!

I propose that you enact a bill that would mandate that marriages last no longer than three years. Include in this mandate that all current marriages on the books are herewith null and void, and that everyone must start over.

Package with this decree a stipulation that will re-write the tax code in a way that will clean up once and for all the sickening interplay between money and love. Enact a law that taxes *all men* 50% of their income, puts the money in a lock box, and pays it out to *all women* on a weekly basis. These changes will allow women the freedom to choose men as they please, without all the anti-quated "good provider" considerations that cloud today's courtship.

Heed the call, WOMEN UNITE, get us what we deserve! Push for this set of laws so we women really can get money for nothing.

Sincerely,

_____ (forge your wife's name here)

146

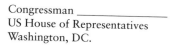

Congressman _____
US House of Representatives
Washington, DC.

Dear Congressman,

Is it rational to believe the same person you marry in your youth will be compatible with you 20, 30, even 40 years later? Hell no! Over that many years anything short of mutual abhorrence is a miracle. That's why most of your esteemed colleagues are divorced now!
    Here's what I want you to do:

1. Enact a bill that would mandate marriages last no longer than three years and make all current marriages on the books null and void.

2. To stifle the screaming women, pay 'em off! Enact a law that taxes men 50% of their income, put the money in a trust fund, and pay it out to women. Hell, we both know that's what's been going on anyway, and 50% is a bargain!

    Forget the WTO, Global Warming, and Campaign Finance Reform! Get off your ass and make some real change for once. Push for this set of laws to strike a final and lasting truce in the war between the sexes.

Sincerely,

_____ (sign your name here)

So get on the Net, call Congress, lobby city hall! With enough pressure in the right places, we can change mankind's outmoded institution of conjugal confinement for the better. If we band together, the future of husbandhood can be a bright, gleaming, Mommy-free place!